Nothi… ole as a Br… en Heart

REFLECTIONS FOR THE DAYS OF AWE

Edited by Simon Eder & Adam Zagoria-Moffet

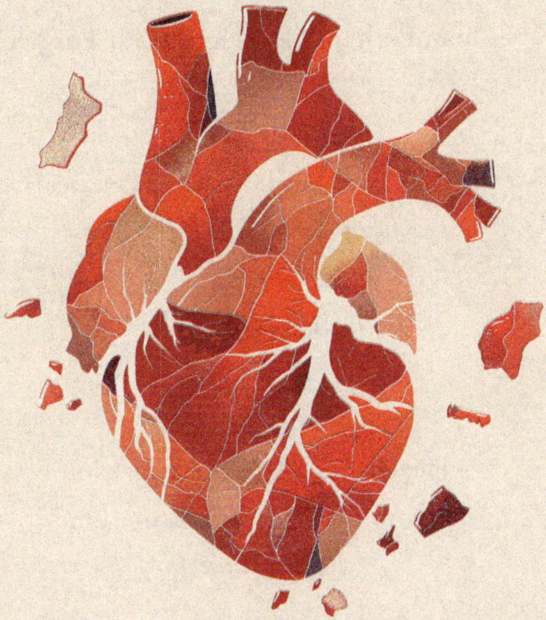

9 781739 089641

CONTENTS

II. ROSH HASHANAH

III. ASERET Y'MEI TESHUVAH

IV. YOM KIPPUR

Why Brokenheartedness?

Adam Zagoria-Moffet

Choosing the title for this volume was difficult. That isn't because of a lack of powerful imagery and compelling phrases in our *machzor* for the Yamim Noraim – we're awash with options! Rather, it was difficult to select a piece of our liturgy that could serve as a title which neither felt too depressing (after all, a key message of the essays herein is hope) nor too flippant (after all, what a year it's been). As a result, we abandoned the *machzor* in our search, sort of.

The Machzor Lev Shalem, published by the Rabbinical Assembly in the United States, called itself such (literally, 'whole heart') in part to play on the famous teaching which is often cited in the name of the Ba'al Shem Tov, but more accurately is that of his later follower, Rabbi Menachem Mendel Morgenstern, the Kotzker Rebbe. The fuller quote seems to be (at least according to Mitchell Morgenstern of kotzk.com):

אין שלם כלב שבור, אין ישר כסולם עקום,
ואין עקום כבדותת יושר (גלייך ווערטל)

> There is nothing so whole as a broken heart, there is nothing straighter than a crooked ladder, and there is nothing deeper than a simple thought.

This idea, and its embrace of the paradoxical,

doesn't originate with the Kotzker Rebbe though, or with Chasidut at all. Instead, it comes from the Zohar, indirectly:

דְּלֵית נְהוֹרָא אֶלָּא הַהוּא דְּנָפִיק מִגּוֹ חֲשׁוֹכָא

> There is no greater light than that light which emerges out of the greatest darkness.
> [Zohar Tetsavveh, 10]

No light is as bright as one that comes from darkness. No heart is as whole as one broken.

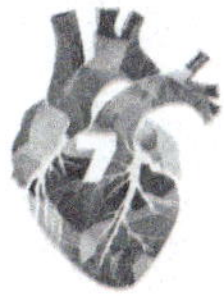

This profound insight seems incredibly appropriate as we aim to balance our desire to commemorate a difficult year for the Jewish people, while also irrepressibly and correctly, looking ahead to a new year and a new start.

Nothing so Whole as a Broken Heart is a collection dedicated to appreciating the contrasts and complexities of the Yamim Noraim. I hope that in its pages you find wisdom and guidance, as well as challenge and provocation. On behalf of the Louis Jacobs Foundation, we are so proud to be able to bring a new generation of Torah scholarship to the public, in keeping with Rabbi Jacobs's oft-repeated maxim that 'the quest for Torah is itself Torah'. So too, the exploration of our brokenheartedness is what heals it and our embrace of the darkness is what illuminates us.

In her essay for this collection, Tova Hartman quotes [Psalm 34:19]: "Adonai is close to the brokenhearted; [God] delivers those crushed in spirit." While she doesn't reference it there, this beautiful verse is given an even more beautiful treatment by the Midrash:

> When a person of flesh and blood has an object, so long as it is whole and intact – they are happy with it. If it is broken, they do not want it. But not so for the Holy Blessed One.
>
> So long as the object is whole, God does not want to see it; but if it is broken then God desires it. And what is the favourite object of the Holy One of Blessing? The human heart.
>
> If the Holy One of Blessing sees a proud heart it is disregarded; as it is said: "Every one that is proud in heart is an abomination to Adonai." [Proverbs 16:5]. But, if it is broken, then God says: 'This is mine,' as it is said, "Adonai is close to the brokenhearted" [Psalms 34:19] [Midrash haGadol 38:1]

Perhaps the best we can ask for this year is for God to be with us in our brokenheartedness, to help us see what the Kotzker suggests: that there is a wholeness in our brokenness which is unparalleled. Just as one who commits a crime but then does *teshuvah* is superior to one who never errs in the first place [Berakhot 34b] – so too – our hearts, when healed, will be stronger and better for having been broken in the first place.

Adam Zagoria-Moffet
St. Albans, UK
Elul 5784

The Journey from Elul to Yom Kippur

Simon Eder

It has been a difficult year, more so than perhaps I can remember in my lifetime. We are all still reeling from the attacks on 7 October, we still await the return of 115 hostages, war rages on in Gaza as many innocent lives have been lost on both sides and of course antisemitism has reared its ugly head in ways unimagined a few years ago. Our world is indeed broken!

There is much about brokenness to which we are invited to reflect during this period.

As we begin reciting Psalm 27 at the start of Elul its words, "Do not subject me to the will of my foes, for false witnesses and unjust accusers have appeared against me" [Psalm 27:12] perhaps seem more pertinent than ever.

Elul's highlight is of course the Selichot service, which sets the tone for the entire period and demonstrates that it is not just the content of our prayers that are important but the haunting music that accompanies them too. For almost three decades I have always accompanied my Dad to the first night of Selichot. We stand together, often in tears as time stands still and the music washes over us!

On Rosh haShanah we dwell on the broken situation so evident from the stories of Hagar and Ishmael, Abraham and Isaac and subsequently Hannah. As Rabbi Wittenberg in his piece beautifully explains, it is the Shofar's *teruah* note which contains all tears – those shed openly as well as those that are hidden.

During those all important days between Rosh haShanah and Yom Kippur, we welcome the chance to reflect upon our broken interpersonal relationships and on Yom Kippur we stand before the Almighty in contemplation about how our paths have veered from the direction originally intended.

The entire season of course, beyond the brokenness, also offers the potential for three important transformations encapsulated by the oft repeated mantra of 'Teshuvah, Tefillah, Tzedakah.' These reach their climax as we stand before our Creator at the Neilah service on Yom Kippur – and the gates of heaven are about to close.

Tzedakah provides the chance to heal our broken world. Tefillah gives the setting to mend our broken selves. Teshuvah at both a societal and individual level is the opportunity to return to our true paths.

It is these themes that our esteemed thinkers, who hail from across the Jewish spectrum, refer to throughout this collection. Drawing on Kabbalistic themes, the singer and poet Leonard Cohen, in his song, Anthem, declares:

Ring the bells that still can ring
Forget your perfect offering
There is a crack in everything
That's how the light gets in.

This volume is then a small attempt to do just that. It is a small attempt to shine a little light in this broken world and accompany us on our own journey during these Days of Awe to healing and at-one-ment.

Simon Eder
London, UK
Elul 5784

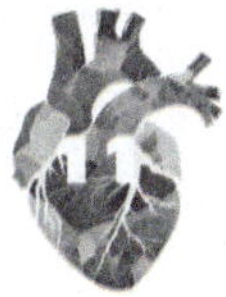

זִבְחֵי אֱלֹהִים רוּחַ נִשְׁבָּרָה
לֵב-נִשְׁבָּר וְנִדְכֶּה אֱלֹהִים לֹא תִבְזֶה

The offerings of God
are a broken spirit –
a shattered and despairing heart
God will not despise

Psalm 51:19

1

Elul

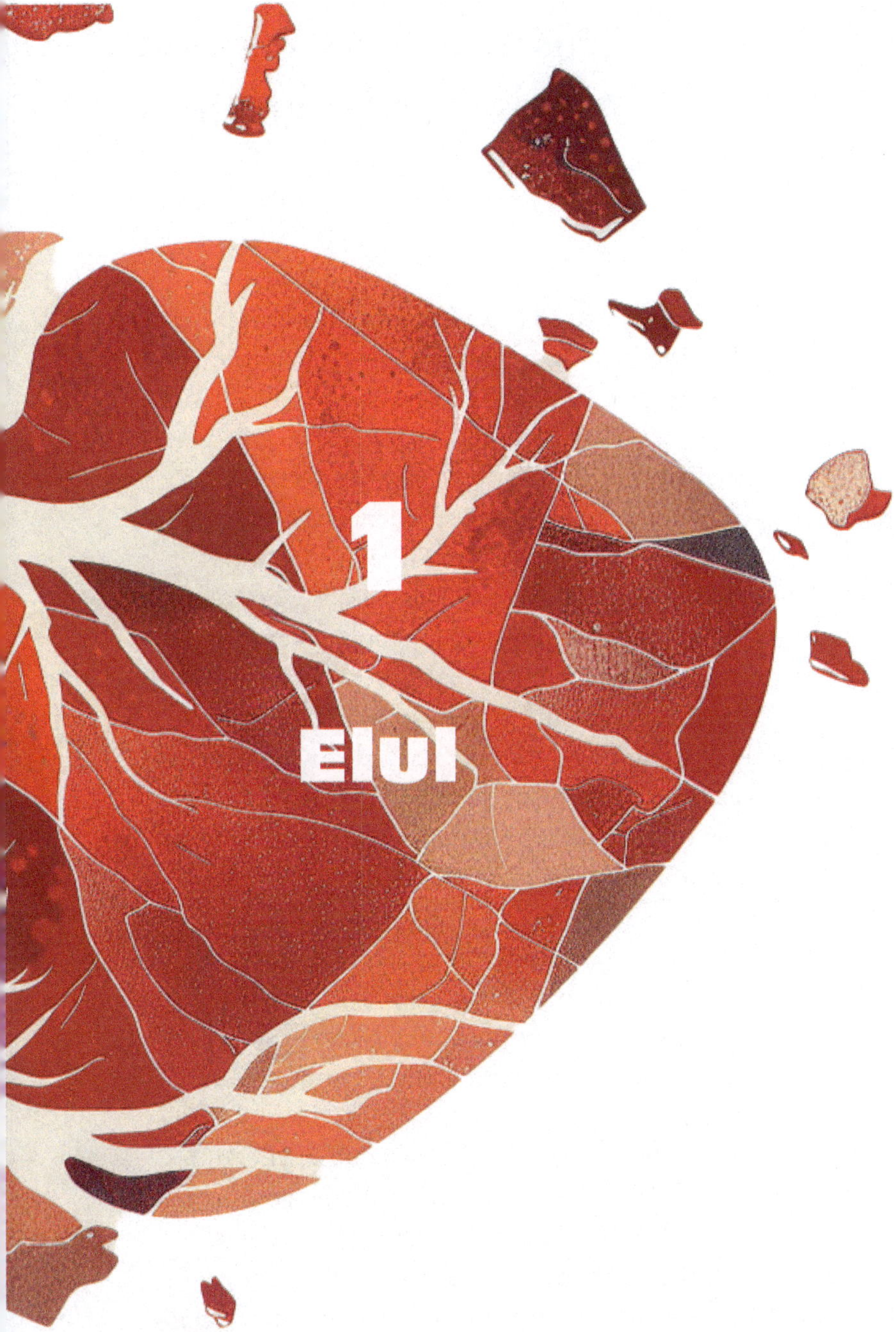

This Year, Perhaps God Needs Our Forgiveness

Yaffa Epstein

This year, Rosh haShanah and Yom Kippur are different - more so than any time in the last 50 years. Almost one year ago, at the culmination of our holiday season – the pinnacle of joy – we experienced the horrific tragedy of October 7, 2023. Since then, we have mourned those who were murdered on that awful nightmare of a day. We have mourned the hundreds who have fallen defending the Jewish people and we have mourned those who were murdered in captivity. We have hoped and prayed for the safe return of the hostages, and we have prayed to see those who were evacuated from their homes return safely to their towns. We have experienced unprecedented hatred from the world around us.

Now, we are about to put on our white clothes, walk back into our synagogues, and pick up our high holiday prayer books. We will spend these days searching our souls, examining our behaviour, regretting the moments when we have not lived up to our full potential. We will confess, beat our chests, and pray to be washed clean of our sins. We will say the familiar *u'teshuvah, u'tefillah, u'tzedakah ma'avirin et ro-ah hagezeirah* – Repentance, Prayer and Charity cause the evil decree to be averted.

Prayer is an essential part of these days of awe. But, this year, there will be a thickness in the room; giant unanswered questions hanging in the air. Hashem – Our God: is it our sins You wish to hear us confess? What about **Yours**? Do You regret the awfulness of this past year? Will You stand in judgement before us?

Shocking and perhaps even heretical questions! Yet there are numerous moments in the Torah where God admits to regretting certain choices, the most notable being the act of creating the human being who had proven to be evil. Of course, the Torah then goes on to tell us that God learns that not all human beings are evil, finding one who is good, Noah, and building an entire world from him and his family.

The Rabbis of the Talmud too, imagine God to be capable of regret. In one of the most moving stories in the Talmud [Babylonian Talmud Tractate Brachot 3a], we are told that Rebbe Yossi, while in transit, stopped into a *churvah* - a destroyed building - to pray. After he had finished praying, Elijah the Prophet appears to him, admonishing him that he should have prayed on the path, and not in a destroyed building!

Elijah then asks Rebbe Yossi: What voice did you hear in the destroyed building? Rebbe Yossi answered him, I heard the voice of the Divine, cooing like a dove, saying "Woe that I destroyed My house, burned My Temple, and exiled my children among the nations." Elijah then responds that this prayer was not only said in the destroyed building but is recited three times a day by God! And further, when the Jewish people enter their synagogues and houses of study to pray, and they praise God's name, God nods in response, and longs for the time when they said those same words of praise in the Temple.

The story highlights that when we are in pain, we want to believe that God too regrets His behaviour. Professor Yoram Hazony understands this story to mean that "God never ceases to regret the destruction he has inflicted upon Israel." *[The Question of God's Perfection]*

There is comfort in being together in the pain.

The text notes that this was not any destroyed building, but one of the destroyed buildings of Jerusalem. We are being shown here the mindset of a people, after the destruction of the Temple and of Jerusalem herself. After trauma, we seek out destroyed places, and we bring our prayers there. If we listen carefully, God can be found in these places of destruction.

Yet, that is not the only place we can find God. The story also mentions another set of buildings – that of the Synagogue and the House of Study. Even after the loss of our most precious possession, the Temple, we responded by creating mini temples in the form of synagogues.

The Jewish People, in their pain and trauma, decided that not all was lost. We created a system of prayer that mimics the sacrifices in the Temple.

While God cries and regrets His decision to destroy, we have the power to rebuild. We have the power to pray.

This year, as we walk into our Synagogues they will hold a dual function for us. On the one hand, they will be *churvot* – destroyed buildings representing all that we have lost. In these destroyed buildings, we are capable of hearing the Divine voice that shares Hashem's pain and regret with us. And they are also *mikdashei me'at*, mini-Temples. Houses that we built, where when God cries, we respond with praise.

Our prayers have the capacity to comfort God, and thus to comfort ourselves. We remind God, and we remind ourselves that we have faith in our relationship. This year, as we pray, may we hold both the pain and the trauma we have endured, find the strength to forgive God, and praise His name.

Days of Awe: An Historical Perspective

Chaim (Harvey) J. Hames

Tishrei is full of festivals, more than any other month in the Hebrew calendar: Rosh haShanah, the fast of Gedaliah, Yom Kippur, Sukkot, Hoshanah Rabbah, Shmini Atzeret and Simchat Torah. Rosh haShanah is not called that in the Bible, but it is מקרא קודש, a day on which the *shofar* is blown "זכרון תרועה". The Bible knows nothing about a day or days of judgement. One must consult the Mishnah to understand how the holy day on which the *shofar* is blown received its current meaning and content.

The opening sections of Tractate Rosh haShanah read as follows:

> The four new years are: On the first of Nisan, the new year for the kings and for the festivals; On the first of Elul, the new year for the tithing of animals; Rabbi Eliezer and Rabbi Shimon say, on the first of Tishrei. On the first of Tishrei, the new year for years, for the Sabbatical years and for the Jubilee years and for the planting and for the vegetables. On the first of Sh'vat, the new year for the trees, these are the words of the House of Shammai; The House of Hillel says, on the fifteenth thereof.
>
> At four times (a year) the world is judged: On Pesach, for the crops. On Shavuot, for the

> fruits of the tree. On Rosh haShanah, all the world passes before Him like sons of Maron, as it says, "He that forms the hearts of them all, that considereth all their doings." (Psalms 33:15) And on Sukkot, they are judged for the water.

Here we find the start of the rabbinical conception that organises the year according to its festivals, noting that there is still a close correlation between the festivals and the agricultural cycle of the year found in the Bible.

The formulation of the second *mishnah* suggests an immediate connection between those festivals and the days on which the world will be judged, and it is noteworthy that these days of judgement are universal and not particular to Jews or Judaism. The Rosh haShanah of Nisan is for all kings and the Rosh haShanah that falls on the first of Tishrei is for the years, the Sh'mittah and the Jubilee which are natural cycles of seven years. The judgement on Passover is for grain in general and that of Rosh haShanah which falls on the first of Tishrei, is for all the inhabitants of the world.

According to the Mishnah, the new year of Tishrei is the day when the year changes, and from this can be concluded that in the view of the Mishnah, it is the day when the world was created and the first year began to be counted. That is, if you connect this concept with the biblical story of creation [Genesis, Chapter 1], Rosh haShanah is the first day of creation, the day when God created the heavens and the earth, began to make order from chaos, differentiated between light and darkness and essentially time as we know it started (in the Midrash, there is a claim that creation began on the 25th of Elul so that the 1st of Tishrei is when man was created – reinforcing the linkage to the concept of the Day of Judgement).

Why, then, did the Tanna'im think to connect between this day and a day on which all the inhabitants of the world are judged? And what exactly is the meaning of "all the world passes before him like sons of Meron"? The rabbinic interpretation, which is expressed in the beautiful description in the prayer ונתנה תוקף, said in the additional prayer of both Rosh haShanah and Yom Kippur, is that of a supreme court where each and every one of us (the Jews) stands trial before God, the supreme judge, and there it is determined "who shall live and who shall die, who is at the end and who is not at the end...".

Repentance or true remorse, prayer, and giving charity can change the evil decree and grant the Jew another year of life. This concept is also strengthened by the language of the Mishnah which identifies and connects the "before Him" with "He that forms the hearts of them all" in the verse from Psalms, i.e. with the one who created man - God.

With the destruction of the Temple in 70 CE and over the coming generations, the Rabbis, who were slowly emerging as an alternative religious leadership to the priestly caste, needed to imbue the festivals with new meanings that would make them relevant for changing circumstances. And so, Rosh haShanah and Yom Kippur became days of awe, and the whole period became one of judgement as our yearly fate is decided by God, a judge who knows our innermost thoughts and judges each person according to her deeds.

Is this diasporic conceptualisation of God as judge and jury of the individual still relevant in a period where there is a new spiritual centre and political independence? Are we not obliged to re-imbue the Rabbinic Jewish conceptions of time, space and being with one more relevant for our current circumstances? For me, living in Israel, there is only one Day of Awe – Yom Kippur. I celebrate Rosh haShanah – not as a day of judgement, but as the start of the new year, a joyous occasion, enhanced by the sounding of the *shofar*.

The days leading up to Yom Kippur are not for reciting S'lichot, but days of introspection about our personal and collective responsibility for the survival and betterment of Israel and preserving the environment (creation) for the sake of future generations. And Yom Kippur is a day of reflection where the act of fasting enables me to shed my physical shackles and concentrate on what is important in the coming year for me, my family, my community, my society, and my country.

This year (5784), however, every day since the massacre on Shabbat and Simchat Torah (7th October 2023) has been a Day of Awe and will continue to be until peace reigns in our country, all the hostages are back home with their loved ones, our soldiers return in one piece from the battlefield, and our country recovers its sanity.

The Religion of the Rabbis

Joel Levy

Pirkei Avot, often translated as *The Ethics of the Fathers* (but literally meaning *The Chapters of the Fathers*) is unlike any other book of the Mishnah. The rest of the Mishnah presents complex literary analyses of different aspects of Jewish law. Pirkei Avot contains pithy, elliptic statements of the condensed wisdom of some of the key rabbis of the tannaitic period, the rabbis of the Mishnah. It is a surprising tract of Jewish 'wisdom literature' sandwiched between volumes on how to co-exist with idolaters on one side and the laws of Temple sin-offerings on the other.

In George Eliot's greatest novel *Middlemarch, A Study of Provincial Life* the troubled central character Dorothea requests the essence of her young friend Will Ladislaw's philosophy of life as follows:

> "What is your religion?" said Dorothea. "I mean – not what you know about religion, but the belief that helps you most?"
>
> "To love what is good and beautiful when I see it" said Will.

In those terms Pirkei Avot describes the 'religion' of the earliest rabbis and it makes for intense reading.

Rabbi Tarfon was a member of the third generation of the sages of the Mishnah. He lived in Yavneh in the tumultuous period between the destruction of the Second Temple (70 CE) and the fall of Beitar in the Bar Kochba revolt (135 CE). Here he is reflecting on his personal 'religion' in Chapter 2 of Pirkei Avot:

(טו) רבי טרפון אומר
היום קצר
והמלאכה מרובה
והפועלים עצלים
והשכר הרבה
ובעל הבית דוחק:

(15) Rabbi Tarfon says:
The day is short
and the work is much,
and the workers are lazy
and the reward is great,
And the Master of the house is pressing.

Rabbi Tarfon is clearly a troubled fellow. He has an excruciating sense of how much there is to do and how hard it is to stay focussed on doing it! We can read his words as relating to the peculiar state of Jewish consciousness that is forever aware of the density of religious obligations weighing us down, not to mention the open ended obligation to master the Torah itself. But he could equally well be referring to the human condition in general; reflecting on how all mindful humans are all too aware of the greatness of the tasks they are set; acquiring an education to understand the world, gaining an occupation to subsist, finding partnership and raising a decent family, contributing to the building of a stable and just society. 'The workers are lazy' – says Rabbi Tarfon, presumably also talking about himself.

None of us choose to carry those weighty existential burdens around with us. We'd rather leave them by the door of the pub, the cinema or next to the TV remote control. Rabbi Tarfon's 'religion' gives him the strength to persist: 'The reward is great' he whispers to himself as he steels himself to pick up his burdens once more. Is he referring to the natural rewards of a life led in pursuit of *mitsvah* and Torah or a life led patiently gaining a trade, acquiring an education, raising a family, seeking social justice? Or does his return to the grindstone require a broader imagined goal and purpose to the whole of existence that would make sense of and justify his daily travails?

What voice, and what message, whispers in our ears when we try to convince ourselves, once again, to recommit to our highest selves and values? The second half of Rabbi Tarfon's 'religion' appears in the next Mishnah:

(טז) הוא היה אומר
לא עליך המלאכה לגמור
ולא אתה בן חורין ליבטל ממנה
אם למדת תורה הרבה נותנים לך שכר הרבה
ונאמן הוא בעל מלאכתך שישלם לך שכר פעולתך
(ודע מתן שכרן של צדיקים לעתיד לבא)

(16) He used to say:
It is not your responsibility to finish the work,
But neither are you free to desist from it.
If you have learned much Torah,
your reward will be much;

and the Master of your work is trustworthy
To pay you the wage for your activity.
(And know, the giving of reward to the
righteous in the future to come.)

We can almost hear the voice of his exhausted interlocutor filling the gap between these two texts. In response to the first Mishnah a tired sceptical voice answers, "You are damn right that 'the work is much', Rabbi Tarfon. It's not just much - it's totally impossible; the mountain we'll have to climb is overwhelming. The Romans are in control; Roman ways of thinking and living have penetrated every aspect of our lives; The Temple, our religious, cultural and legal centre has been destroyed; Jewish intellectual life is in ruins and only a sorry few of us are trying to rebuild our cultural infrastructure from scratch; our people are dispersed over the known world so our economy is in tatters; and you call this 'the work is much'!"

Let's pause to list for ourselves the huge challenges facing our world as we approach her annual M.O.T. in 2024! The feeling of the immensity and complexity of those challenges confronts us as never before in our generation. But our awareness of those challenges so often pushes us away from serious engagement rather than towards it.

We silently offer thanks for the somewhat crumbling genteel bubble that we have managed to construct for ourselves. We inwardly convince ourselves that merely watching the news and taking a stance on the problems facing us constitutes a significant engagement

(The Achilles' heel of the chattering classes); we distract ourselves with the pleasantries and toys that we have accumulated; and we excuse ourselves with words that echo the voice of Rabbi Tarfon's *bar plugta,* his imagined interlocutor; 'the work really is too much – so pass the G and T'.

But Rabbi Tarfon's responses stop us and him in our tracks. "It is not your responsibility to finish the work, but neither are you free to desist from it", he insists. Stop hiding behind the complexity and immensity of the challenges. You have a small part to play, but a part to play nonetheless. And if that is not enough then remember that "The Master of your work is trustworthy to pay you the wage for your activity".

Our contributions are not a meaningless drop in the ocean, but a noticed and meaningful part of the world. Almost all sane humans follow a religion, in Dorothea's terms. We choose to live by a creed that it actually matters how we manage to behave. Although we may mouth the idea that life and morality is meaningless, none of us would dream of following that as our religion, as 'the belief that helps us most'.

So this year during the ten days we will try, together, to prise open the words of Rabbi Tarfon and explore where we have attempted to immunise ourselves and close ourselves off from the weighty tasks in hand.

Hearing the Voice of Fair Zion, from Lament to Consolation

Rachel Adelman

Tishah b'Av commemorates the greatest tragedies that befell the Jewish people, including the destruction of the First and Second Temples (in 586 BCE and 70 CE), as well as repeated expulsions and pogroms throughout Jewish history. To these I would add the most recent events of October 7th, though clearly the dates do not coincide. In one day, more than 1,200 men, women, and children (most of whom were civilians) were killed by Hamas terrorists, over 250 were captured and held for ransom in Gaza, often in appalling conditions. As I write today, 120 are still held in captivity, many likely no longer alive.

That 'Black Sabbath' Day shocked the Jewish people and Israel, comparable only in recent memory to one day of mass slaughter during the Shoah. In the wake of October 7th, I feel compelled to hear the women's voices—those who survived the onslaught of terrorists and/or captivity in Gaza, as well as those who did not.

In Eichah, the feminine personification of Jerusalem, Bat Tzion—often translated as "Fair Zion" — speaks directly out of her brokenness, her *shever*, to protest her degradation [1:9b, 11b-15a, 16, 18-22; 2:11-12]. While she admits to her transgressions [Lam. 1:14, 22], to having rebelled [vv. 18, 20], in the end she is, in the words of King Lear, "more sinn'd against than sinning." The prophet Isaiah later vindicates her: "she has received at the hand of the LORD double for all her sins" [Isa. 40:2].

Throughout the scroll, both the narrator and Daughter Zion cry out that there is no one to comfort her [Lam. 1:2, 9, 16, 17 and 21]. One of the dominant definitions of 'comfort' in its ritual sense is to assume the state of mourning alongside the mourner. Yet Daughter Zion stands alone, overlooking the devastated city, as a witness to the terrible suffering of her children; there is no one to stand with her. Even when the narrator offers to comfort her, with the rhetorical question: "What can I compare to you so that I may console you, Dear Maiden Zion?" [Lam. 2:13], she spurns his offer and takes up the dirge [vv. 20-22]. Only God can be her comforter. Perhaps, the entire book of Lamentations may be read as a call for God to comfort Zion. Yet God is silent in the scroll. There is profound lament and a searing plea but no divine answer.

The most poignant response to the un-answering is found in the oft repeated motif of comfort and compassion in the prophecies of Isaiah. In the weeks that follow Tishah b'Av, all seven *haftarot* of consolations are taken from the latter chapters of Isaiah. The series opens with the command: "Comfort, O comfort, my people, says your God..." [40:1]. This call is reinforced, when the prophet asks: "Who will grieve with you?... how shall I comfort you?" [51:19, echoing the narrator in Lam. 2:13]. Later, she is called the "not comforted one" [Isa. 54:11]. God announces that He alone will be the comforter: "I, yes I, am He that comforts you..." [51:12].

What can we do today to provide comfort to Bat Tzion? How do we respond to 'the Devastation' in the wake of October 7th, when the divine answer to her plea is muted, even silent? Perhaps simply by our hearing, our bearing witness to her devastation and mourning with her, we participate in the process of healing, and thereby offer some comfort to her, who poignantly had 'none to comfort her'. I take seriously the questions in [Lam. 2:13]: "How can I bear witness for you? What can I liken to you?...How can I comfort you?....Who can heal you?" For me, they are not rhetorical but genuine interrogatives about how we approach trauma in the biblical text, as in life. In the words of Theodor Adorno: "The need to lend a voice to suffering is a condition for all truth."

As a sequel to this reading of Isaiah and Lamentations, I offer a new midrash written in the wake of October 7th, composed by Liora Eilon, a member of Kibbutz K'far Aza, where more than sixty residents were slaughtered and at least eighteen were kidnapped. Liora, a seventy-year-old mother of four, grandmother of seven, was held up in her sealed 'safe room' for over thirty hours, with her son, daughter-in-law, and two granddaughters, while her other son, Tal Eilon, along with others from the home guard, battled the hundreds of Hamas terrorists that overwhelmed the kibbutz. When she was finally released from her safe room, Liora found out that

Tal had been killed. She recounts her story (in Hebrew) on YouTube. But the following *midrash* tells her story in another way. Like Bat Tzion's voice in Lamentations, she articulates a call for compassion. Her piece is inspired by the second verse in Eichah, depicting Bat Tzion crying alone at night. It asks, as does the rabbinic *aggadah*: why does she cry alone at night? What impact does her weeping have? But then Liora Eilon challenges the Rabbis, who would have the woman removed from the neighbourhood so as not to disturb the great Rabban Gamliel [Talmud Bavli Sanhedrin 104b].

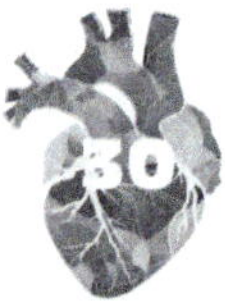

The Power of a Community to Diminish Suffering in the World

Liora Eilon

Cry, she will cry at night *(bako tivkeh ba-lilah)*...
[Lam. 1.2]

'At night.' For all who cry at night, one who hears their voice, cries along with them.
[Talmud Bavli Sanhedrin 104b]

'Cry, she will cry *(bako tivkeh)*' [Lam. 1.2] – this is none other than a command: you will cry *(tivkeh)*! One must cry in response to the sorrow of one's neighbour, whose son or daughter has died. For thus one takes away a little of their sorrow and places oneself a little in their place.

At night *(ba-lilah)* – One must cry in response to the sorrow of one's neighbour, whose son or daughter has died. For thus one takes away a little of their sorrow and places oneself a little in their place.

At night *(ba-lilah)* – for in the daytime their neighbours see their grief and may cry with them. At nighttime, people are left alone with their grief, and this is why it is written 'Cry, she will cry *(bako tivkeh)*' (in the emphatic form), so that their neighbour cries with them at night, and as the weeping and sorrow are shared, they are diminished a little in the world.

There was a woman who was Rabban Gamliel's neighbour, whose son died and she would cry for him at night. Rabban Gamliel heard her voice and cried along with her until his eyelashes fell out. The next day his students took note and removed her from his neighbourhood. [Talmud Bavli Sanhedrin 104b]

But Rabban Gamliel was fulfilling what was written 'cry, she will cry at night' [Lam. 1.1], so why did they remove her from his neighbourhood? His students said, because his eyelashes fell out – and that was because he was crying alone. His neighbours didn't hear him crying, and didn't cry along with him for the one who lost her child. That's why we removed her from the neighbourhood....

[Translated from the Hebrew by Yehudah Mirsky]

Liora Eilon continues the meandering thought-path of classical *midrash*, comparing the woman bereaved of her son to Abraham, who was like a sealed flask of balsam oil [Genesis Rabbah 39:2]. God commanded the patriarch to "Go forth *(lekh lekha)* from your land and your birthplace and your father's house..." [Gen. 12:1], in order to spread the word of ethical monotheism.

So too the students moved the woman from her neighbourhood so that, like a bottle of perfume uncorked, she could trail the scent of her sorrow and stir compassion in others. Thus Rabban Gamliel would not cry alone for her at night, but the entire Jewish community [here identified as Knesset Yisrael, the feminine collective and sequel to Bat Tzion] would weep with her at night. Her voice would become "like a shofar sounding from one end of the earth to another."

When we hear the cry of the Shofar this holiday season, let us also hear the broken sobs of the bereaved mother, and of all those whose dear ones are still held in captivity. And let us cry with them so that the weeping and sorrow are shared, and so they are diminished a little in the world.

How to Heal That which Is Broken in 1...2...3

Jeremy Gordon

So much feels broken. I'm forever stepping on shards. There's pain from the pain, and there's pain from surveying all this brokenness. But Rosh haShanah is coming. So here are the three lessons I am trying to hold as close to my heart as I can.

1. *Change is possible*

There is an incredible optimism at the heart of Rosh haShanah. Our past does not absolutely govern our future. I know only a naïve fool does the same thing over and over expecting a different result, but I still hope. My hope – our hope? – is not yet destroyed. I believe, as Theodor Zeldin wrote, that, "History, with its endless procession of passers-by has so far largely been a chronicle of waste. But next time two people meet, the result could be different. That is the origin of anxiety, but also of hope and hope is the origin of humanity."

The second two lessons are harder.

2. Teshuvah requires letting go of the certainty of our own merit.

It's tempting to believe we are stronger by conceding nothing. But it's not an appropriate response to the call to *teshuvah*. At this time of year, we are called to focus not on the appalling failures of the other, but on our account. At other times of the year, it's possible to construct every occasion when we reach out a hand as utterly genuine, and every failure of the other to shake our hand as their perfidy. But on Rosh haShanah we are called to ask what we could have done differently. It's a necessary focus because we rarely heal, or even normalise, relationships with others by increasing our focus on quite how right we are.

3. We must let go of our claim to totality

This is the opening of the Mishnah in Bava Metzia:

> Two people come before the court grabbing hold of the same *tallit*. One says, 'I found it and it's all mine.' The other says, 'I found it and it's all mine.'

You see the problem? Intractable. They both claim the whole *tallit*. They both want to be acknowledged as right, but their claims are mutually exclusive. Having presented the challenge, the Mishnah continues to teach us that you get both to swear an oath that not less than half of the *tallit* is theirs and then you split it in half.

Rabbinic Judaism offers a solution that appeases both claims even as both are forced to compromise. Both make an oath which they can agree with. Then both get less than they hoped for, but more than they feared losing.

Interestingly the Mishnah shows no interest in working out, Solomonically or otherwise, exactly who did get there first. Rather we are directed towards a way out of intractable mutually exclusive claims where we both get less than we hope, but more than we feared losing. There is always that third way.

May we seek it, may we find, may we never give up looking for it.

A Cord of Hope

Shai Held

The Days of Awe are a time of hope, predicated upon the possibility of transformation and renewal. The essence of *teshuvah*, we are taught, is that we ourselves, our families, our communities, our people, and the world as a whole are capable of being more than we presently are, of doing more than we presently do. The day will come, we are promised, when human dignity will be real and the presence of God will be manifest.[1] Then (and only then) will God be fully recognised—and crowned, as it were—as God.

There are times when such transformative hope seems almost totally inaccessible. This is, sadly, one of those times. Both Diaspora Jewish communities and Israel are faced with profound existential crises, and the possibility of redemptive transformation seems remote at best. So many of us are bewildered and exhausted. Hope? Renewal? Transformation? The words fall flat.

So what can we hold on to as the Days of Awe approach?

In a provocative image, the talmudic Sage R' Abbahu imagines that God created and destroyed multiple worlds before creating the one we now inhabit [Bereishit Rabbah 3:7]. Commenting on this midrash, R' Joseph Soloveitchik[2] strikingly observes that "here we have God not only creating, as in the Biblical text, but also recreating, rebuilding after destructions." Why is this important? Because, R' Soloveitchik suggests, the way God is portrayed here is meant to teach us a profound ethical and spiritual lesson: "As God creates and recreates... so too, should [human beings] be ready to rebuild and reconstruct, even as previous structures collapse." This is not easy, Soloveitchik admits: "To build initially is difficult, but to rebuild is even more challenging."

Faced with destruction and devastation, we are nevertheless "bidden to start over again with faith and resourcefulness, as God did. ... This, then, is what the Torah requires of [human beings]: to act, to create and, when necessary, to recreate, even as did the Divine Creator."[3] To be tasked with being God's partner, in other words, is not simply to be presented with raw materials and told to build. It is, at least some of the time, to be confronted by horrible loss—by confusion about the past and uncertainty about the future, by the temptation to succumb to despair and fatigue—and to somehow manage to choose life instead.

And yet that choice can feel—and be—so hard. To buoy myself lately, I have been reflecting on the Hebrew word for hope, *tikvah*, which also means 'thread,' as in the phrase *tikvat chut ha-shani*, the cord of crimson thread that Rahab hangs outside of her window as a sign for Joshua and the Israelites to let her family live [Joshua 2:18]. I find myself thinking: sometimes hope is little more than a very slender thread, but that thread is everything, almost literally salvaging life from

the grips of death.
A verse in Job reflects on the hope suggested by a tree:

איוב יד:ז
כִּי יֵשׁ לָעֵץ תִּקְוָה
אִם־יִכָּרֵת וְעוֹד יַחֲלִיף
וְיֹנַקְתּוֹ לֹא תֶחְדָּל׃

Job 14:7
There is hope (*tikvah*) for a tree:
if it is cut down it will renew itself;
its shoots will not cease.

A chopped-down tree may look dead, but under the surface there is the possibility of more life. This same hopefulness is captured by a verse in Isaiah using an almost identical metaphor to foretell the messianic redemption:

ישעיה יא:א
וְיָצָא חֹטֶר מִגֵּזַע יִשָׁי
וְנֵצֶר מִשָּׁרָשָׁיו יִפְרֶה׃

Isaiah 11:1
A shoot shall grow out of the stump of Jesse,
a twig shall sprout forth from his roots.

Perhaps this is our task: to affirm (to insist) that, even if much of what we care about most is hanging by a thread, growth, change, and renewal can (will?) yet come.

We should not confuse hope with optimism. I am not optimistic, but I am hopeful—at least some of the time. If anything, the literary critic Terry Eagleton writes, "hope and temperamental optimism are daggers drawn." The point Eagleton is making is profound and essential. Optimism, he says, is "a form of psychological disavowal... a moral evasion"; it "does not take despair seriously enough." Perhaps counterintuitively, optimism is thus "the enemy of hope, which is necessary precisely because one is able to confess how grave a situation is." So what is hope? It is, in the philosopher Paul Ricoeur's wonderful phrase, "a passion for the possible"; it is, Eagleton explains, "a movement toward the good, not simply a craving for it."[4]

In other words, hope involves commitment.[5] So as we enter these days of reflection, let us examine both our lives and the world in which we live them, and let us grasp for the cord of hope, however slender and vulnerable it may be.

During the Days of Awe, we recite a wonderful phrase that is as elusive as it is evocative: *ha-yom harat olam*, which is often translated as 'today is the birthday of the world.' But in Hebrew, *herayon* refers to pregnancy rather than birth. So, with some homiletical licence, I suggest that this year, even amidst our grief and our worry, we translate as "today is pregnant with the (possibility of a renewed) world."

Amen, ve-khen yehi ratzon.

[1] See Micah 4 as a poignant example of this.
[2] 1903-1993.
[3] R' Joseph B. Soloveitchik (ed. Abraham Rav Besdin), *Reflections of the Rav* (1979), pp. 28-29.
[4] Terry Eagleton, *Hope Without Optimism* (2015), pp. 5, 11-12, 52.
[5] Wanting things to change without committing to help making them change is wishing, not hoping.

2

Rosh haShanah

Is It Okay to Love Life?

Bradley Shavit Artson

On July 16, 2006, a bearded Hezbollah guard was quoted in the Los Angeles Times. He said: "People are begging Hassan Nazrallah to fight. They want to be human bombs." Then he added the following comment: "This is the difference between us and them – the Jews. They fear death and love life; we are believers in another life, and we welcome death." Jews fear death and love life, he says. I am not prepared to concede that this guard speaks for other Muslims – I suspect they love life very much. But I will admit that when it comes to the Jews and their love of life, I think he is right.

Is it terrible to love life? Hezbollah thinks it is. They think this will make Jews look bad. Those Jews - they are afraid of dying because they love life so much. Is that a sin? Does it reflect a lack of faith to love life?

> Who is it who desires life and loves many days to see good, keep your tongue from evil and your lips from speaking guile. Depart from evil and do good. Seek peace and pursue it [Psalm 34]

Jewish tradition understands that loving life is not a self-indulgence. To love life is a mandate to do good and to flee from evil. To love life is to pursue peace and to spread it among our brothers and sisters. To love life is to see life arrayed before us as a feast, a bounteous party to which we are invited guests. The Talmud commends to us:

> Grab and eat. Grab and drink. Because this world from which we will one day depart, is like a wedding celebration, a wedding feast [Eruvin]

We were – all of us – born into a world that was created for us. In the creation story at the beginning of the Book of Genesis, we are told that humanity was made, not at the beginning of creation, but at its end, to which the rabbis comment that just as when one celebrates a party, one sets up the party first, and then tell the guests to come so it is that God arrayed this glorious pageant of beauty: water and land; sky and sea; animals and plants; bedecked the world and festooned like it a glorious banquet, and only then beckoned us to join. How can one not love life if we understand that the world is a wedding feast?

Each day that God creates the world, God says, *'Ki-tov'* – 'It's good!' And then stepping back at the end of Creation and looking at it all – even that exclamation is not enough. God says, *'Ki-tov me'od'* – 'It's very good!'

Rav Saadya Gaon teaches, "the first of God's acts of kindness to God's creatures was the gift of life." Judaism affirms that life is a gift. To spurn the gift is to spurn the one who gives it. How dare a religious person not love life? How dare a person who claims to be God's servant throw the gift back at God? As the Holy Day Machzor reminds us, "You who remember life, remember us in the Book of Life."

Jewish law, Halachahh also emphasises again and again that loving life is a supreme religious value. The Talmud tells us that nothing stands in the way of saving a life other than three prohibitions. Because living itself is a mandate. Again the Talmud tells us, "When there are two legitimate ways to interpret Jewish Law, one of which makes possible living, then you are obligated to rule leniently." The Torah tells us, "You should live by them." The Gemara goes on to explain, "You are not commanded to die by *mitzvot*." The laws of the Torah are meant to enhance life, to add to the beauty of the world we are born into.

My guide in the love of life is my son. At the time the Hezbollah article appeared in the Times, Jacob was a 14 year-old boy enrolled in the local public Middle School. As he has grappled with the world's responses to autism his whole life, Jacob has taught me what it means to love life. Here is what Jacob wrote as a response:

> For most of my life my existence was controlled by autism. Autism was at the root of every experience I had or didn't have. I lived with constant anger at my disability and fear that it would isolate me forever. One day last year, my wonderful physician and mentor asked me, what is the opposite of anger? And I realised that it's not the absence of anger, but rather acceptance, laughter, and joy. I also realised that fear and anger just produces more fear and anger, while acceptance brings connection to God and humanity. For many years I have been praying for God to cure my autism, and wondering why God didn't answer

> my prayer. I realise now it is because I have been praying for the wrong reason. I started to pray for the strength to accept Autism and to live with joy, laughter and connection. My prayers have been answered more richly than I could have ever imagined. I still passionately hate autism, but now I love life more than I hate autism.

Is that not the life-task of every human being? To move from fear and anger to acceptance and joy?

Anger is a trap. Anger ensnares us in its reach and then won't let us ever leave. Small wonder that the Talmud says: "One who tears garments in anger, who breaks utensils in anger, or scatters money in anger, that person should appear to you as though performing idolatry," for anger is the craft of the *yetzer hara*, of the evil inclination.

A letter written by the Baal Shem Tov, the founder of Hasidut says, that when tempted by anger, which is an expression of sinful fear and derives from the attribute of judgement, overpower your inclination and transform that trait into a chariot of God. Make your fear and your anger, which are expressions of weakness, into a chariot for God, a vessel for the sacred.

An ethic which takes creation seriously bids us to tell the Hezbollah guard that his anger and his fear have warped him; have robbed him of his humanity, and are a betrayal of the very religious convictions that his own religion teaches. I have read the Koran. I have seen the life-affirming teachings that can be found there for those who look. But, first, one must leave aside fear; step beyond hatred. And I say this to myself, to all of us, because we too become trapped in our fear and our hatred and our anger– and it is paralysing. To move beyond anger into joy is the work of a lifetime and it begins each day.

An 18th century poet, William Elory Channing tells us:

> To live content with small means,
> to seek elegance rather than luxury,
> and refinement rather than fashion;
> to be worthy, not respectable,
> and wealthy, not rich;
> to study hard, think quietly,
> talk gently, act frankly;
> to listen to stars and birds, babes and sages
> with open heart;
> to bear all cheerfully, to do all bravely;
> await occasions and hurry never.
> In a word, to let the spiritual,
> unbidden and unconscious
> grow up through the common,
> This is to be my symphony.

The Torah mandates: "You shall rejoice before God." And it is precisely that command to rejoice that sets us free. In Jewish mystical thought we are told that what we do in this world below has an impact in the world above. And when we release the bonds of rage, the bonds of depression, the bonds of fear, the trap that it must always be like this, we liberate supernal joy as well.

Reading the Book of Records

Jeremy Tabick

The *piyyut* Unetaneh Tokef refers to 'the Book of Records' which 'reads itself' before God and has 'the seal of every person in it.' What is this book and what is it trying to teach us about the way we should live our lives?

The idea for this Book derives from a tradition of Rabbi, the towering leader of his generation of sages toward the end of the tannaitic period, preserved in the last line of a very rich *mishnah* in Pirkei Avot [2:1].

> ... and all of your deeds in a book are written.

Rabbi's book is not merely a list of names, like the Book of Life and the Book of Death. Rather, the Book of Records contains a chronicle of all of your deeds. This is the book that, in Unetaneh Tokef, is opened and being read before God, like a text-to-speech app.

Looking at the fuller context of Rabbi's *mishnah* gives us a nuanced idea of what this image is supposed to accomplish for us: it is supposed to affect our actions. Here is the entire *mishnah*:

> Rabbi says:
> What is the straight path that a person should choose?

1
Anything that is beauty to the one who does it
is beauty for them from other people.

2
And be as careful with a lenient *mitzvah*
as with a stringent *mitzvah*,
because you do not know
the gift of the reward of *mitzvot*.
And be evaluating the loss of a *mitzvah*
against its reward,
and the reward of a sin against its loss,

3
Look at three things and you will not come
into the power of sin.
Know what is above you:
An eye seeing
and an ear hearing
and all your deeds in a book are written.

All three sections of this passage emphasise that we are limited in both our knowledge and our power. We do not know the details of how we will be punished or rewarded for our actions.

Similarly, the road to the straight path and to avoid sin is to remember what is above us, that all of our actions are noticed and recorded, that there is a power beyond ourselves.

We imagine that we are evaluating what is good or bad for us based on our own cost-benefit analysis, but in truth we cannot correctly predict what will be the effects of our actions. Only God truly knows what is good.

Even the first part of Rabbi's advice, which focuses on our actions in relation to other human beings, makes a version of this same point. We might think that our own internal sense of what is right and wrong should be the final arbiter when deciding our actions. But this is just pride.

In fact, when we make choices we need to consider both how it seems to us and how it will seem to others. Certainly our own inner life provides an important voice to us, but it does not define what is good, but is in a complex negotiation between us, others, and God.

The *mishnah* in Sotah [9:15] concisely attributes to him exactly the qualities that he was trying to inculcate in his advice in Avot:

> When Rabbi died,
> humility and fear of sin ceased.

Rabbi's tradition in Avot is deeply related to the two qualities he was known for most of all: humility and fear of sin. We see this humility in both narratives about Rabbi and in his interactions in Halachic conversations. The very first time Rabbi[1] is mentioned in the Mishnah [Kilayim 2:11], he disagrees with an anonymous, majority opinion, after which he says:

> I agree with your words more than my own.

In other words, the very first thing Rabbi does in the Mishnah is to concede to his opponents. 'I originally thought that this was right,' says Rabbi, 'but I was open to the majority wisdom and, having thought about it, came to the decision that I was wrong, that my own agency and decision-making would have led me to the wrong outcome if it were not for the input of others.' This is Rabbi living out his advice in Avot: not only do you need to think that something is the right decision, but it needs to be recognisable as such also by others.

What does this have to do with the fear of sin, Rabbi's other distinguishing quality? This is exactly what his advice in Avot is about: humility leads to the fear—or perhaps better: avoidance—of sin. If I approach every decision thinking about how others will judge my actions, or how God will write about it in the Book of Records, then I am helping myself to limit my actions within the bounds of what is good and right. Consequently, I will be less likely to make mistakes and sin. If I do not assume that I have all the answers or all the information, but that I am missing a perspective that I can uncover with further reflection or consultation with others, I will end up coming closer to the truth.

The next time you have to make a difficult decision, think about what it would be like to read your account in the Book of Records. Would you be proud? Embarrassed? Puzzled? Did you do the best you could, taking into account as many perspectives as possible in order to get as close to the best outcome as you could? And even if you think you did your best, would that come across to someone else reading the account?

This is the exercise Rabbi wants us to do, and the attitude that the image of the Book of Records is supposed to help us cultivate.

I hope that all of us this year can be known—like Rabbi—for our humility and fear of sin.

[1] In the printed edition of the Mishnah, this is R' Meir, but it is clear from the mediaeval manuscripts, preserving a more authentic reading, that this is supposed to be Rabbi.

Is Loneliness a Desert?

Natasha Mann

I am reconsidering the desert.

I've long considered the desert in biblical texts to be the place of raw creation. It is, after all, where revelation seems to occur the most. But I was fortunate enough to hear Dr. Karolien Vermeulen of the University of Antwerp reframe the desert in psychogeographical terms, and this description brought two High Holiday narratives together in my mind.

The first is the narrative behind the Unetaneh Tokef's poetic depiction of a great *shofar* sounding and a *kol d'mamah dakah* (a still, small voice) being heard. The story itself is from 1 Kings 19. The Prophet Elijah flees from society into the desert in a state of great distress, his life threatened by a murderous regime. He is ready to give up, but God will not let him. An angel visits Elijah in the wilderness, sustains him with food and water, and leads him through a prophetic vision into a new understanding of the divine. First comes a great wind – but God is not in the wind. Then, an earthquake – but God is not in the earthquake. Then, a fire – but God is not in the fire. And finally, a *kol d'mamah dakah*, a still, small voice.

Elijah's story is clearly using Moses and the revelation at Mt Sinai as a thematic backdrop. The resounding silence of God is a subversion of the overwhelming theophany of Sinai. But there are significant differences to their wilderness experiences. First, it's a different desert; Elijah flees into Be'er Sheva.

And even beyond the physical location, the psychogeographical location is different.

Moses was not alone in the Sinai story. He was surrounded by his people, aided in leadership by his siblings, and his path was set by the divine presence. Elijah entered the desert physically, emotionally, and spiritually alone.

Many centuries beforehand, someone else walked into that same desert. Someone else was visited by an angel to be questioned and nurtured and redeemed. Someone else went from experiencing the desert as the backdrop of despairing solitude to the place of meeting God.

On the first day of Rosh haShanah, we read about the complicated interpersonal relationships that lead up to the Binding of Isaac. Hagar is the victim of this first story. She and her young son, Ishmael, are cast into the wilderness. For Hagar, though, this is a second lonely experience in the desert. Her first time in the lonely desert was when she was pregnant, having fled the mistreatment of her mistress. In that first version of the desert narrative, Hagar sat by a source of water and was approached by an angel.

"Where have you come from, Hagar, and where are you going?" the angel asked her. ("*Mah l'kha fo, Eliyahu*?" the angel would later ask the prophet. "Why are you here, Elijah?")

This interaction culminates in a divine promise about offspring that could rival those given to the patriarchs. Emboldened and comforted, Hagar would return to the camp, but not before enacting her own kind of blessing: she gives a new name to God. El-Roi, she names God; 'the God Who Sees Me'.

Our Torah reading is of Hagar revisiting the location of her loneliness. In Genesis 21, she is cast into the desert instead of fleeing. She is no longer physically alone; she carries her young child with her. When the water runs out, having found no alternative source, Hagar places the child in the shade and she lifts her voice and cries out. The God Who Sees Hagar returns to her for another scene of redemption. This time, the angelic question is: *Mah lakh, Hagar?* What is to you?

It does not escape me that the question, *mah lakh,* sounds like the word for angel: *mal'akh.* Much is made of the angel telling her not to be afraid and to lift up the child, but I wonder if this poetic play could be the angel's *hineini* ('here I am') in response to her cry.

This time, when Hagar is sustained with water and promises and blessings, she remains in the desert to raise her child.

With the benefit of the Prophet Elijah's story, I see something new in Hagar's. Her first time in the lonely desert, Hagar doesn't think to cry out. She simply goes there and waits, silent in her solitude. This second time, however, she lifts her voice. This Hagar is cast into a dark and lonely place, a situation that will likely lead to death not only for her but for her precious child, and she lifts her voice and cries out.

Perhaps the first Hagar is like the Prophet Elijah. She has given up. The wide nothingness of the desert is the backdrop of her loneliness and lack of hope. But this second Hagar is the one who has learned what Elijah needs to be reminded of: that God is there in the quiet, too.

Placing these two characters side-by-side highlights that hearing God in the lonely desert is not simply about factual knowledge. Of all people, the Prophet Elijah should know that he is not truly alone. It is about an awareness that lives in the heart instead of the mind.

That, I think, is the type of knowledge that Hagar gains when she gives God a name. The God Who Sees Me. This is the same kind of lesson that Elijah learns through the soft murmur in the silence. In both stories, perhaps loneliness is only a desert when we aren't ready to hear God in the great silence.

May all lonely deserts be so transformed.

A Silence Between

Samuel Klein

"Music is not in the notes, but in the silence between."

Depending on whom you ask, some version of this could have been said by Mozart, Claude Debussy, Miles Davis, or an anonymous Zen monk.[1]

Regarding the latter, for centuries, Japanese aesthetics has paid close attention to negative space in a concept called Ma, which literally means a 'gap', 'interval,' or 'pause.' Briefly outlined, Ma is considered 'empty intervals of space or time' that invite some sort of action to fill them with meaning. Ma is not created by individual compositional elements of a building, a drawing, or a piece of music, rather it is the space between the walls, the white between lines on paper, and the silence between sounds, essentially 'non-form, non-line, or non-sound.'[2] It is what occurs in the imagination during a given experience, particularly with a work of art, but more broadly with life events. Any meaning attached to form or occurrence pools into the silences or 'voids' between the design elements or the unfolding action.

間

In the Western classical tradition, it is Beethoven who emerges as *primus inter pares*, first among equals when it comes to grappling with silences. What had hitherto been known in musical notation since the early 15th century as a Fermata, a technical pause of unspecified length, was now an actual motif. For Beethoven, a 'nothing' could be just as expressive as a 'something,' and therefore could be deployed well beyond its purely functional use as a 'period,' or 'rest' between movements; it was now woven into the very fabric of his art. And what emerged, what echoed in the stillness, all depended on the predominant emotional tone and register of a particular composition.

Whether you are sitting in a concert hall, or listening on Spotify, it is difficult not to be jolted by his explosive, searing silences; for example, his overture to Coriolan or most famously, the first movement to his Eroica Symphony. Right away, there is a build-up of unprecedented ferocity, the pace relentless. We wait, predicting the resolution or 'final drop' we know is just around the corner. But when we reach the downbeat of measure 280, Beethoven abruptly suspends the heroic momentum, and we sense the conductor's hands suspended motionless, holding what Grosvenor Cooper and Leonard B. Meyer declare as "the loudest silence in musical literature."[3]

How long this fermata is sustained is up to the interpretation of each maestro. And in the case of Eroica, there have been performances where those hands have in mid-air for more than four beats—an almost unbearable 'cataclysmic' silence at the core of the opening movement.

Let us imagine our reading of Akedat Yitzchak (the Binding of Isaac) on the second day of Rosh haShanah, was set to a musical score—an extended symphony to match the epic scale of Eroica or the Coriolan overture. In the sheet music, accompanying Abraham and Isaac on their ill-fated journey to Mount Moriah, might be this very same devastating fermata, mirroring what is quite possibly (to borrow from Cooper and Meyer) the 'loudest silence' in Hebrew Scripture:

> 6 Abraham took the wood for the burnt
> offering and placed it on his son Isaac, and he
> himself carried the fire and the knife. And the
> two of them went on together.
> 7 Then Isaac turned to Abraham and said,
> "Father?"
> "Yes, my son?" Abraham replied.
> "We have the fire and the wood," the boy said,
> "but where is the lamb for the burnt offering?"
> 8 "God will provide a lamb for the burnt
> offering, my son," Abraham answered. And
> they both walked on together.
> [Genesis 22:6-8]

There it is. A gaping void signified simply by an unassuming 'comma.' What dread things rush in to fill that space! Here is no minute interval between a variance in pitch. More frightening than the clash of steel on steel or sounds of a brutal cavalry charge, is the terror of what is not said between this parent and his child:

> "God will provide a lamb for the burnt offering, my son."

The biblical commentator Radak amplifies the desperate ambiguity in the text. Abraham's response to Isaac supports two equally valid interpretations. The first: 'Don't worry, God already knows where we will find the lamb for the offering. He will place it at our disposal.' The second: 'God will select the lamb for the offering; and who is to be the lamb? It is you, my son.'

The first response is a hint, perhaps even, as Gersonides suggests, a desperate prayer seeking to discover an alternative to the horror. The second, delivered unadorned and with crushing clarity. Both suggest a dark and unconscionable intent.[4]

As if to mute the agony of our scene, the Torah quickly adds: "and they continued walking on together," which the Targumim, the earliest translations of the Hebrew text into colloquial Aramaic, have as, "And they went both of them in heart entirely as one".[5] Of course, we have already encountered the refrain just a verse earlier, and it wasn't very convincing there, either.

But, whatever is intimated by the repetition, we are to be reassured that Isaac is now whole with the path forward. He doesn't falter or stumble, or run screaming from the mountainside. Instead, father and son are in lockstep, are "of one heart and one mind" in doing what needs to be done.

And what of Isaac's age? For the mediaeval rationalist Abraham Ibn Ezra, it is of crucial importance to establish that Isaac, on hearing his father's reassurances, is no naive stripling of 5 years, skipping along, oblivious, at his father's heels for the three-day journey toward certain death. That would undermine the integrity and gravity of his question. And yet, neither is Ibn Ezra convinced by rabbinic tradition that Isaac would have been a grown adult of 37, since, "Scripture passes completely over Isaac's own pious self-sacrifice and submission to Divine Will, which surely would have been worthy of mention." Ibn Ezra, therefore, has Isaac as a youth of close to 13 years, allowing for his seemingly precocious intuition but also keeping Abraham as the principal actor in the drama, who is aware of what is really going to happen.[6]

George Segal, Abraham and Isaac (In Memory of May 4, 1970, Kent State University), 1978, The Jewish Museum, NY.

On the question of Isaac's age, sculptor George Segal, commissioned by Kent State University in 1978 to memorialise the four unarmed students protesting the war in Cambodia who had been shot and killed by the Ohio National Guard, appears to have sided with Ibn Ezra.

In *Abraham and Isaac In Memory of May 4, 1970, Kent State University (1978–79),* Segal depicts Isaac as a youth, kneeling before Abraham, knife in hand and poised to deliver the killing blow. It was a controversial choice of narrative for a memorial to what came to be known as the Kent State Massacre. University officials refused the sculpture, alleging that it glorified the violence of Abraham's act.[7]

In early 2022, visitors to the Jewish Museum in New York were able to see for the first time the original life-sized plaster sculpture, 40 years after the controversy surrounding its installation at Kent State.

The curators of *Personas: George Segal's Abraham and Isaac*, the exhibition mounted to explore the secondary material generated by the controversy, focus the dramatic lighting in the galleries on Abraham standing on a rock, knife drawn, over the kneeling and bound Isaac. On the walls around these figures are the voluminous fragments of correspondence: letters, notices, photographs, newspaper clippings detailing the events of 1978-79; the request to adjust the sculpture and the artist's subsequent refusal which led to the University's refusal to install the commissioned work. Ironically, this eventuality might have been commentary itself to Genesis 22: the charge to create, to move, to act in the world and the rescinding, or rather voiding of that very charge by those who gave it.

Segal's sombre ensemble, more void than presence, is in some ways anticipated by German-

Jewish philologist and critic Erich Auerbach, who in his sweeping study of 'Western' literature in Mimesis, draws our attention to the negative spaces rife throughout Genesis 22.

Contrasting the textual hyper-colour of Homer's Odyssey and particularly the hero's homecoming in Chapter 19 (where the roving spotlight of the narrator foregrounds every move and choice of the protagonists), Auerbach understands the Akedah as taking place amid the shadows with our text vague and understated, so much unseen and unsaid:

> Only the decisive points of the narrative are emphasised, what lies between is non-existent; time and place are undefined ... thoughts and feelings remain unexpressed, are only suggested by the silence and fragmentary speech; the whole permeated with the most unrelieved suspense ... and directed towards a single goal, remains mysterious and 'fraught with background'.[8]

The terrain is colourless and flat, with no signs of life, save the muffled footfalls of Abraham and his kinsmen on the road. The singular moment of betrayal of everything hallowed by Abraham is made all the more stark against the blurred contours of the main story line. I believe Auerbach would concur with the musical analogy offered earlier, likening this journey to "... a holding of the breath, a process which has no present, which is inserted, like a blank duration between what has passed and what lies ahead".[9]

We might imagine, as on the downbeat to measure 280 of Beethoven's Eroica, that the 'biblical score' demands that the conductor's arms grow heavy and weary holding this fermata. It needs to feel unbearable. In paying close attention to this oppressive and suffocating silence within a silence, we might be accompanied by another German-speaking Jew, Holocaust survivor and poet, Paul Celan.

Celan's poetry is known for its dramatic thematizing of the interplay of absences and pauses between words. Although without knowledge of the precise circumstances under which he wrote and written though they may have been for another time and context, here are his words, which ring true for me as if overheard between our two silhouetted figures set against Auerbach's grey landscape 'fraught with background' on a mountainside cloaked in mystery and awe:

> Speak, you too,
> speak as the last one,
> have your say.
> Speak--
> But do not separate the no from the yes.
> Give your saying also meaning:
> give it its shadow.
>
> Give it enough shadow,
> give it as much
> as you know to be parcelled out between
> midnight and midday and midnight.
> Look around:
> see how alive it gets all around-- At death!

Alive!
Speaks true, who speaks shadows.
But now the place shrinks, on which you stand
Whereto now, shadow-stripped one, whereto?
Climb. Feel yourself upwards.
Thinner you become, unrecognisable, finer!
Finer: a fathom
along which it wants to descend, the star:
to swim down below, below
where he sees himself swimming: in the swell
of wandering words.[10]

In Celan's poem, *Speak, you too*, the language folds into itself. Is it one calling to another? Is it the meandering of a slowly unravelling mind? Perhaps a soliloquy delivered looking out toward a distant horizon line? It is unclear, ambiguous. And then, there is that comma, perhaps signalling a dramatic pause of indeterminate length, our fermata! Which is left to the reader's discretion. How long to pause? How long to leave words suspended?

By hedging his language with this pause, Abraham is successful in calming Isaac's growing sense that something is awry. Yet, this recalibration of Abraham's, his subterfuge, also reveals a momentary wavering, a pitch of uncertainty in this disquieting music—is this actually all a ploy? Does God really want him to rebel, to disobey?

> "And Isaac spoke to Avraham, his father, and said: My father" [Gen. 22:7] Samael (Satan) came to our father Avraham and said: "Old man, old man! Have you lost your mind?! Do you truly intend to slaughter the son given to

> you at the age of a hundred!'" 'Indeed so,' he replied. [Samael said:] 'And if He sets you an even greater test, will you be able to stand it?!' [as it is written:] "Because he tried you with one thing, will you be weary" [Job 4:2]? [i.e are you capable of withstanding larger trials? Is there no limit to your obedience? Will you comply with any command?"] 'Yes, even more so,' he replied. Samael said, 'Tomorrow He will call you a murderer and say you are culpable for shedding your son's blood!' He replied: 'Still I go'.[11]

Midrash Rabbah is one among numerous iterations of similar trope—Satan remonstrating with Abraham—which rushes to fill the void behind us as the biblical score begins a new movement toward the final resolution: Abraham is about to commit a terrible, monstrous crime, that of murder. This is the tremendum of the Binding of Isaac: the upending of a life lived with valour and grace and setting in its place a sordid and spineless capitulation. Even Satan comes out looking good here.

Abraham has spent his entire life fighting on the side of the angels, not the beasts, and now in a sickening re-enactment of his traumatic brush with death by fire as a younger man, he is leading his own son, clueless into the flames?

As if in response to this theme, I am struck by the ash-coloured funerary tones of Segal's sculpture, and, shown in situ (below) it is almost as if both father and son have been overtaken by the sudden rush of the pyre prepared before them and charred to a cinder where they both stood and knelt. Abraham doesn't escape the fiery furnace at Babel after all. His trauma is too deeply rooted.[12]

In 'Fear and Trembling,' what is by now one of the great philosophical commentaries on this episode, Soren Kierkegaard cuts at the elegance and dignity of the Hebrew text, all the way through to the bone: God told Abraham to commit murder, and Abraham obeyed, cheerfully, quietly, faithfully—and for this, in the Bible, he is praised?!

> "If faith cannot make it a holy act to be willing to murder his son, then let the same judgement be passed on Abraham as on everyone else. If a person lacks the courage to think his thoughts all the way through and say that Abraham was a murderer, then it is certainly better to attain this courage than to waste time on unmerited eulogies. The ethical expression for what Abraham did is that he meant to murder Isaac; the religious expression is that he meant to sacrifice Isaac—but precisely in this contradiction is the anxiety that can make a person sleepless, and yet without this anxiety, Abraham is not who he is."[13]

Kierkegaard's midrashic overture, delivered as four parts in the exordium at the opening of his book, lends colour and texture to the terse exchange between father and son. In the first of these, rather than upend Isaac's faith, Abraham intentionally takes the fall, sacrificing Isaac's view of his father's own humanity, while simultaneously reinforcing his son's belief in an All-Merciful God. But under the weight of this pretence, Abraham's unwavering faith in a just and compassionate God is suffocated alongside his conscience right there on the mountainside:

> "... Then Abraham turned away from him for a moment, but when Isaac saw Abraham's face again, it had changed: his gaze was wild, his whole being was sheer terror. He seized Isaac by the chest, threw him to the ground and said, "Stupid boy, do you think I am your father? I am an idolater. Do you think it is God's com mand? No, it is my desire." Then Isaac trembled and cried out in his anguish: "God in Heaven, have mercy on me, God of Abraham have mercy on me; if I have no father on earth, then you be my father!" But Abraham said softly to himself, "Lord in Heaven, I thank you; it is better that he believes me a monster than that he should lose faith in you."[14]

On a personal note, and writing as a parent, it is so very hard to resist the powerful urge to move from dissonance to consonance, to resolve the dynamic tension of "Father?", with a chocolate-box-and-red-ribbon closing (and there are a good number of such redemptive closings to be had). But the chordal patterns in this movement of our

Biblical score do not allow for any such artifice. Instead we are dragged to the cliff edge and our faces held over the abyss with the wind howling in our ears. This then, is the musical composition of the Akedah, the disturbed tonal palette hovering above a gut-wrenching question:

> But now the place shrinks, on which you stand
> Whereto now, shadow-stripped one, whereto?
>
> - *Speak, You Too*, Paul Celan

1. With grateful thanks to David Isenberg for our discussion about the consolations of music and for bringing this quote to my attention.

2. Arata Isozaki, quoted in *Ma: Japanese Time-Space,* The Japan Architect 54, no. 2 (Februrary, 1979) p.71. I first came across this idea when learning more about composer Toru Takemitsu's score for the film 'Ran,' Akira Kurosa's stunning retelling of King Lear, and his careful use of silence (also present in many of his concert works). In the first battle scene, for example, Takemitsu provides an intense extended passage that pulls up short at the sound of a single gunshot, leaving us the audience with the sudden rush of the sounds of battle; the screaming, neighing, and fighting. It is well-documented that Takemitsu considered Debussy among his compositional mentors. See: Donald, Richie, *Notes on the Film Music of Takemitsu Tōru,* Contemporary Music Review, vol. 21, iss. 4, 5–16 (London, 2002)

3. Quoted in Grosvenor Cooper and Leonard B. Meyer, *The Rhythmic Structure of Music* (Chicago, 1969) p.139. For a broader discussion of the theme of silence in Beethoven's music, see: Barry Cooper, *'Beethoven's Uses of Silence'* in The Musical Times Vol. 152, No. 1914 (Spring 2011), pp. 25-43 and also: Daniel K.L. Chua, Beethoven and Freedom (2017).

4. Mikraot Gedolot, Commentary of R' David Kimchi, S.V *Vayomer Elohim Yireh Ha-seh Le-olah Beni.*

5. Targum Onkelos Genesis 22:8 (ad loc).

6. Commentary of R' Abraham Ibn Ezra, s.v *Ve-Kidmuneinu* (ad loc).

7. George Segal as quoted on the Princeton Campus Art webpage. After eight months of negotiation, Kent State University declined Segal's project. In December 1978, the Mildred Andrews Fund, which had commissioned Segal's sculpture, offered Abraham and Isaac to Princeton University. The following year it was cast in bronze and installed there.

8. Erich Auerbach, 'Odysseus' Scar' in *Mimesis: The Representation of Reality in Western Literature* Trans., Willard R' Trask. Princeton, 2003) p.11.

9. Erich Auerbach, ibid., p.11

10. '*Speak, You Too*' in Paul Celan, Selections. Edited and with an introduction by Pierre Joris (2005) p.54

11. Midrash Rabbah 56:4. For similar versions of this midrash, see: Samuel A. Berman, trans., *Midrash-Tanhuma-Yelamdenu: An English translation of Genesis and Exodus* (Ktav, 1996) p. 144, (Vayera 22) and B.T. Sanhedrin 89b.

12. For further discussion about the echoes of Abraham's abuse at the hands of Nimrod see: Avivah Zornberg, *The Murmuring Deep* (2009) p.202: "The fiery furnace and the father who kills two sons become the foundational narrative of his life. In a sense, the Akedah is the inevitable confrontation, the test, that is to define his inner world."

13. Soren Kierkegaard, *Fear and Trembling,* trans., H. Hong and E. Hong (Princeton, 1989). p.30

14. Soren Kierkegaard, ibid. (1989). In the selected entries from Kierkegaard's Journals and Papers included as supplementary addenda to the Hong translation, we notice that in a first draft (Pap. IV A76.28), Kierkegaard used somewhat different language: "I imagine that Abraham first of all looked at him with all his fatherly love, and his crushed heart and venerable countenance made what he said more urgent; he admonished Isaac to to bear his fate patiently [...] – but it did not help. I imagine that then Abraham turned away from him for a moment and when he turned back to him again, he was unrecognizable to Isaac, - his eyes were wild, his expression chilling; his venerable locks bristled like furies upon his head ..."

The Brokenness at the Root of Jewish Prayer

Tova Hartman

The Jewish people are mourning incomprehensible devastation and loss amidst our untold individual traumas and collective tragedies. Engulfed in disillusion, we are confronting the murderous rage of our enemies. The religious and political rifts already threatening to tear our communities apart before October 7 are nearing a point of rupture and the vitality of our collective spirit is being tested.

Against the widespread delegitimisation of Israel and normalisation of antisemitism, we are all fighting for our Jewish future, but treading different paths—often with unyielding intolerance for any other. We have lost the good faith of *Eilu v'Eilu*, of honouring our differences. It is not just unity that we lack. We are pervaded by mistrust, suspicious of one another's intentions.

The pain we each feel at this precipice of uncertainty is profoundly subjective and while there is no definitive roadmap for repairing our fractured unanimity, as Jews we traditionally find comfort in shared prayer. Praying together with our hearts broken offers our most efficacious entreaty to God: in the words of the psalmist, "Adonai is close to the brokenhearted; [God] delivers those crushed in spirit" [Ps 34:19].

In our brokenness, as we come together in *tefillah* on Rosh haShanah and reflect on the unprecedented challenges and upheaval of the past year, how do we reconcile the dynamic ineffability of our personal anguish and prayers with the fixed, scripted words of the *machzor*?

The sages who codified Jewish law understood that a standardised set of prayers could not encapsulate the religious, spiritual, and existential exigencies of every individual, nor reflect our subjective experiences. The paradigm for Jewish prayer in the Babylonian Talmud is gleaned from the biblical story of Hannah [1 Samuel 1-2], whose spontaneous, mumbled supplication, recited on the first day of Rosh haShanah, became the template for our liturgical laws and ethos. In her unspeakable brokenness, Hannah's devotion was canonised, and we learned to pray.

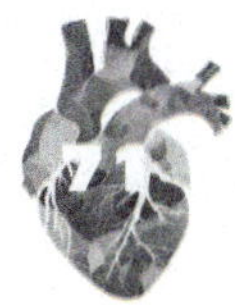

What was it in Hannah's story that captivated the rabbis' spiritual imagination? What rendered the quality of voice in her desperate, unintelligible plea a paradigm for prayer, intimating for the sages the very nature of what it means to call out to God?

In the biblical story, Hannah's disturbed affect in the midst of a sacrificial feast proves unsettling to her husband Elkanah, who asks, "Hannah, why do you cry and why do you not eat?" When the feast ends, Hannah goes alone to the Temple—conspicuously choosing a public place of worship over the privacy of her tent—and "in her wretchedness, she prayed to the Lord, weeping all the while."

At this moment of intense personal prayer, we learn that Hannah is being watched by the High Priest Eli from an exalted perch "upon his seat by the door-post of the Temple of the Lord."

Literally and figuratively, Eli is looking down on Hannah from a position of power. Hannah's lips are moving, but she utters no words as she has no voice to externalise her prayer. Eli cannot recognize her devotion and in his ignorance reproves her for being drunk.

How did the very biblical character whose prayer was ineffable become the archetype for structured Jewish worship? Each statute of the Talmud corresponds to a verse [Berachot, 31a-b]:

> "And Hannah spoke in her heart..." (one must have conscious intention in prayer)
> "...only her lips moved..." (one must enunciate with the lips while praying)
> "...and her voice could not be heard..." (prayer must be recited silently)
> "...so Eli thought her to be drunk" (a drunk person is not permitted to pray).
> "And Eli said to her: How long will you remain drunk? Remove your wine from yourself" (one who observes another's improper behaviour is obligated to reprove).

After putting the rules of prayer into place, the sages continued to give voice to Hannah's intentions, characterising what they heard as defiant subtext in her seemingly deferential reaction.

"And Hannah replied, 'Oh no, my lord!'" Ulla said, and some say it was R' Yossi the son of R' Hanina: "She said to him, 'You are not a master in this matter, and the Divine Spirit does not rest upon you, that you suspect me of this thing.'"

This Talmudic imagination builds on the biblical verses. Here, Hannah observes Eli doing something highly improper—humiliating her in a misuse of the statute to reprove others—and she calls him out for his abuse of power. The audacity attributed to Hannah is striking. She challenges the High Priest's divinely sanctioned authority and infers that his insensitivity in misreading her intent betrays in him an inner spiritual bankruptcy. 'You are not a man of God.'

What the Bible presents as the narrative denouement to Hannah's story, the Talmud dwells on as a thematic summation with a central religious message. For the rabbis, Hannah's personal prayer initiates a process through which authority figures may be critiqued for failing at their positions—making it a legal imperative both for those who have been wronged to speak up, and for the authorities guilty of such abuses to placate those they have hurt. This process of social criticism and cultural self-correction is so integral to the sages' understanding of Hannah's story, to the essence of prayer itself, that they encode it as a natural extension of its derived laws.

When standing before God, the sages taught, we must actively recognize all who stand beside us and acknowledge that there are many individuals in the communal experience. The brokenness in our people cannot be repaired if we do not stop to seek out and understand one another's pain. On the High Holy Days, we immerse ourselves in traditional prayer and give voice to that brokenness, creating a religious embrace to dovetail with one another's faltering speech.

Hannah exemplifies what psychologist Carol Gilligan calls 'a different voice,' one that is often silenced, marginalised, and even pathologised. These voices may not be represented in our Machzor but they should be welcomed as core to our liturgical tradition and need to find a place in our communal religious lives. If in its quest for piety, our rabbinic leadership is incapable of accepting differences in subjective expression, according to the rabbinic depiction of Hannah, they are not genuine individuals of God and we are not a community of God or prayer.

Murder and Redemption

Tzemah Yoreh

In one of my recent books I employed the provocative title: *Why Abraham Murdered Isaac*. The provocation is not the notion that Abraham killed his son. That has been offered as an alternative ending to the story since the early Midrash as illustrated by Shalom Spiegel, but rather the use of the word 'murder' to describe the act. With the choice of that word, I am rendering a moral judgement upon our patriarch and accusing him of high crimes.

The freedom to say what one thinks is sometimes employed by my fellow rabbis as a prerogative to impose their own values upon the text and argue that *that* is what the text really says. Academics would refer to this with an appropriate nine-letter word (more impactful than a four letter word), as eisegesis – 'reading into the text' – the evil twin of exegesis. I am absolutely fine with eisegesis as long as one admits to it from the outset. Eisegesis serves a vital function of keeping the text fresh and relevant for a new generation of readers.

In the canonical text of Genesis 22 a merciful and loving God stays Abraham's hand and prevents Isaac's sacrifice. Or are we reading love and mercy into the text? There are many other motives one could attribute to God here. The motive I find most plausible is that having tested

Abraham's faith, God is interested in preserving the continuity of Abraham's line, a line of faithful worshippers.

From Rabbinic Midrash through recent theological discourse there has been an attempt to ground the notion of a Jewish 'God of Love' in Jewish text. I don't find this God in Tanakh.

He may be located in early Christian literature, and some strata of Rabbinic literature, but a divine Lord of Love is almost entirely absent in the Hebrew Bible. There are many God characters in these 929 chapters. There is the God one should be afraid of, because any approach to him is dangerous, there is a remote God who created both Good and Evil, there is a God who plays dice as in the Book of Job, there is a God who is unsure of himself as in the Garden of Eden and the Tower of Babel, there is a localized God who joins Israel for the ride through the desert and the promised land, there is the deistic God of Ecclesiastes, and there are many more.

Pirkei Avot encourages us הֲפֹךְ בָּהּ וַהֲפֹךְ בָּהּ, דְּכֹלָּא בָהּ. Or in the words of my *Doktor Vater* Israel Knohl, there is a divine symphony in the pages of the Tanakh.

In Deuteronomy, God is described as loving Israel a number of times, at least the root א.ה.ב is used, but as has been argued by my teacher Moshe Weinfeld, the Book of Deuteronomy is structured as a vassal pact between an overlord and his subjects. In this context the root א.ה.ב is best translated as loyalty and obedience.

Don't get me wrong, I entirely sympathise with the search for a loving God. If I were inclined to believe in a personal God, I would certainly want him to love me. I just don't find him in the Jewish texts which are most important to me, and do not think we should impose him upon our canon, as much as he would be a panacea for our pain. Personally, I cannot locate him at all in the cold harsh world after the Holocaust.

I, especially, do not find him in Genesis 22.

In my title, *Why Abraham Murdered Isaac*, I deliberately impose my modern humanist value system on the text of the Hebrew Bible. Today, anybody who upon hearing voices kills his son on a mountain would be convicted in a court of law as either criminally insane or as a first-degree murderer, depending on the judge and jury. In my book the reason for the murder is perhaps even more disturbing, I try to show that according to the original account in the Book of Genesis, Abraham did not fear God or trust him in his encounter with Abimelech the King of Gerar in Genesis 20. This led him to present his wife as his sister, and consequently Sarah was taken into the house of Abimelech, who likely impregnates her. To atone for this sin of mistrust Abraham is required to demonstrate a higher degree of '*yirat elohim*' and is commanded to sacrifice this son. This he does in the first version of the tale. He murders Isaac.

What is the moral of this first version for the modern reader? We must evince fear and trembling of a non-Kierkegaardian variety as we consider this account. It is a terrible tale, and its ramifications have been profound. This version of the story was used by our ancestors to justify the murder of their own children during the crusades, lest they be converted to Christianity, and that is but the tip of the iceberg. I see this story as a cautionary signpost never to use faith in God in ethical debates. Claims from faith are unfalsifiable. We have no way to test if those who say them are true prophets or not.

And thus on the High Holidays I would end with this famous story from Buber's *Tales of Hasidim*:

> A clever student asks "What lesson can we learn from atheists? Why did God create them?"
>
> The Rabbi responds "God created atheists to teach us the most important lesson of them all – the lesson of true compassion. You see, when an atheist performs an act of charity, visits someone who is sick, helps someone who is in need, and cares for the world, he is not doing so because of some religious teaching. He does not believe that God commanded him to perform this act. In fact, he does not believe in God at all, so his acts are based on an inner sense of morality. And look at the kindness he can bestow upon others simply because he feels it to be right."
>
> "This means" the Rabbi continued "that when someone reaches out to you for help, you should never say 'I pray that God will help you.' Instead for the moment, you should become an atheist, Imagine that there is no god who can help, and say 'I will help you.'"

Tears

Jonathan Wittenberg

'What can you hear in this note?' I ask the class at our Gan Alon pre-school, as I blow the nine short mini-tones of the *teruah*, sounding the *shofar* gently so as not to frighten the children. They offer all kinds of answers, from falling leaves to the footfalls of elephants. But to me the *teruah* cry emerges from the *shofar* like tears, rolling one by one down raw cheeks.

There are many tears in the liturgy of Rosh haShanah. Some we hear clearly. Hagar lifts up her voice and weeps as she watches her young child Ishmael dying from thirst, before God's benign angel intervenes. Hannah sheds tears every year, when her husband brings gifts for the children of her rival wife Peninah, but she remains childless. The prophet Jeremiah foresees Rachel weeping for her descendants as, centuries later, they go down into exile, where, by the rivers of Babylon, they too will weep.

Other tears we are never told about, like those we can imagine Sarah weeping with anguish, when she hears how Abraham has taken their beloved son up the mountain to the sacrifice. The *shofar*'s *teruah* contains them all, the tears wept in secret and those shed openly. Indeed, the Talmud describes the nine short sounds as *yevavot*, taking the word from the cries of Sisera's mother when her son, the great general, fails to make his usual triumphant return from battle because he lies dead at the feet of Yael. It's as if to say: even the tears of grief of your enemy's mother are still tears in God's eyes.

I don't know what to say about the fact that these are all tears of women, and all of them about children. Maybe we men are too stubborn-hearted to cry. Or, more likely, we shed our tears in secret, not wanting to let on that we too have the need to weep.

5784 has been a wretched year of bitterly painful tears. When I met the father of the dancer, 23 year-old Romi, still held hostage, and Ayelet, mother of Naama, just twenty and also still captive to Hamas in Gaza– they did not weep.

Nor did the family I visited whose son was killed while successfully protecting the new recruits in his army base on October 7. In public, these remarkable people showed their courage, determination and humanity. But in private their tears must be endless.

I did witness the tears of others, Iris who wept for her community whose children had to go to battle, and for her beloved country in trauma; Yael, who wept for all the hopes of peace, for all the friendships she had carefully nurtured beyond all political borders and religious divides, and which were now, too, the victims of hatred and war. I heard, too, via radio and television, the tears of mothers in Gaza.

There's a prayer we say just before the close of Yom Kippur which has always been important to me:

> May it may be Your will, O God who hears the sound of weeping, to store our tears in the flagon of Your heart and protect us from all further harsh decrees.

This year, those words, always poignant, are the very soul and guts of the prayers of the whole community of Israel. They reach far beyond, to Ukraine, and so many other places in a world, directly or by proxy, at war.

'Stop your voice from weeping, and your eyes from shedding tears,' God tells Rachel in Jeremiah's vision. 'For the children will return from the land of the enemy and in your future lies hope.' I pray that these words come true long before Rosh haShanah and that the year ahead will bring consolation and hope for all Israel, all humanity and all life.

Should Abraham, Sarah, and Hagar Do Teshuvah?

Naomi Graetz

Post Traumatic Stress Disorder (PTSD) is a topic that is surfacing now in Israel with the 50th anniversary of the Yom Kippur War of 1973. We listened recently to the story of an Israeli prisoner of war, who was captured in the early days of the war, saying that every night he still has nightmares about the Egyptian officers who tortured him, both mentally and physically. A few years ago I wrote an article called *Trauma and Recovery: Abraham's Journey to the Akedah.* I periodically visit this article, twice a year in fact, when we read the story of what I call the two sacrifices of Abraham's sons, Ishmael and Isaac.

Now I can just hear the critical reader saying, why use the word sacrifice for Akedah, which means binding. However, whether Abraham actually sacrificed his son Isaac, which some mediaeval sources claim he did, or not, there is no way that he did not sacrifice his relationship with both sons.

Every year I practise reading the Rosh haShanah texts with its special trope. I really know it by heart after reading it for about forty-five years, but I love the special melody and each year I see something that I haven't noticed before. This year it was the expression על אודות בנו that caught my eye. By coincidence I had just finished reading *Althea: The Life of Tennis Champion Althea Gibson* by Sally H. Jacobs, at the same time that Coco Gauff won the U.S. Open in tennis. In the biography, the author depicts the horrendous physical abuse and privation that Gibson suffered as a child and how it affected her entire life. Gauff, who has a sense of history has paid homage to the Williams sisters and to Gibson.

I have thought a lot about how Abraham and Sarah both needed to do *teshuvah* because of the way they treated their children. It starts with Sarah's telling Abraham גרש את האמה הזאת. She treats Hagar, her maid/servant/slave, as זאת—a thing, an object. Her reasoning is that the son of the 'thing' האמה הזאת should not inherit together with her son, with Isaac. The Hebrew is exquisite here. Because in contrast to Sarah's seeing Ishmael as a non-person with no rights, Abraham sees him as his son: וירע הדבר מאד בעיני אברהם על אודות בנו.

Obviously the 'thing' דבר is bad in his eyes concerning 'his son', presumably Ishmael, but it will leave scars on the other son, Isaac who no doubt loves and admires the big brother who plays with him. Unfortunately for Abraham (and obviously Hagar and Ishmael), any thoughts of acting upon these bad feelings concerning his son, are dispelled by God, who tells him to listen to Sarah, and even tells him not to feel bad about the expulsion. Banishment, displacement, and relocation are big themes in the bible-starting with Eden and ending with Exile.

Rather than protest and put a stop to this, Abraham goes along with this sacrifice. We can only sense, like with all primal stories (think the Brothers Grimm), the horror of what is being done to the child. The Bible does not directly relate to it; perhaps it hints at it.

And this of course, sets him up for the next chapter, when Abraham goes along, blindly without any protest to take his remaining son, Isaac to be slaughtered. There is no protest at all. It's almost as if Abraham is too ready to do what God will ask him.

> Sometime afterward, God put Abraham to the test, saying to him, "Abraham." He answered, "Here I am" (הנני). "Take your son, your favoured one, Isaac, whom you love, and go to the land of Moriah, and offer him there as a burnt offering on one of the heights that I will point out to you." So early next morning, Abraham saddled his ass and took with him two of his servants and his son Isaac. He split the wood for the burnt offering, and he set out for the place of which God had told him [Gen 22: 1-2].

Whereas, when Sarah told him to send Hagar and Ishmael away, his reaction was 'it was a very bad thing in Abraham's eyes, concerning his son', here we have total apathy. In fact, we even have eagerness, if we look at the word *hineni*—here I am–at the beginning of the text. Is it blind obedience, or a numbness, a sense of inevitability on Abraham's part? But then he repeats *hineni* right before Isaac asks him about where the lamb is for the burnt-offering [22:7-8]:

> Then Isaac said to his father Abraham, "Father!" And he answered, "Here I am, my son-- הנני בני." And he said, "Here are the firestone and the wood; but where is the sheep for the burnt offering?" And Abraham said, "It is God who will see to the sheep for this burnt offering, my son בני." And the two of them walked on together.

At this point Abraham clearly recognizes that it is his son (notice בני is mentioned twice), and reassures him like a good father should. But this will also be the last time they walk together again—after the big betrayal that is to come.

The word *hineni* appears once more, right before the angel calls to him:

> They arrived at the place of which God had told him. Abraham built an altar there; he laid out the wood; he bound his son Isaac; he laid him on the altar, on top of the wood. And Abraham picked up the knife to slay his son. Then a messenger of יהוה called to him from heaven: "Abraham! Abraham!" And he answered, "Here I am." "Do not raise your hand against the boy, or do anything to him. For now I know that you fear God, since you have not withheld your son, your only one (יחידך), from Me."

Clearly Abraham has forgotten (or is in denial) about his other son, the banished one, both physically and it would seem mentally as well, for he does not comment on the angel's words. It is interesting that JPS translates the word יחידך as 'favoured' son. Just imagine Isaac's last glimpse of his father with knife upraised coming down on him and hearing his father say 'Here I am';. He thinks: Who is he here for? Certainly not for me, his son!

For me, the modern reader, it is exquisitely painful to see how children are pawns in the story.

> Abraham took some bread and a skin of water, and gave them to Hagar. He placed them and the child on her shoulder, and cast her out (וישלחה). And she wandered about in the wilderness of Beer-sheba.

Perhaps had Hagar not gotten lost in the wilderness, she would have survived. But Abraham forgot to give her a compass--and he certainly lacks a moral compass! Perhaps there was some hope that they would both die. Sure enough the story continues:

> When the water was gone from the skin, she cast the child (ותשלך את הילד) under a bush.

Notice how, just as Abraham cast her out (*shelach*), she casts (*vatishlach*) the child, not her son. In order to do this, she had to objectify him as well.

> And then she: went and sat down at a distance, a bowshot away; for she thought, "Let me not look on as the child dies." And sitting thus afar, she burst into tears.

Even when she can no longer bear the sight of his suffering and burst into tears, far away from him, she refers to him as the child (הילד). One wonders how she could possibly bear the thought of his dying alone without holding him. Even though she avoids hearing his suffering, God hears his voice and calls out to Hagar and points out where there is water and that he will be blessed in the future.

Both she and Abraham are rewarded for their passivity in the face of their children being sacrificed for a greater cause. But they both have much to answer to their children who in the future will never forget their trauma. Is Isaac still on the altar?

No where in the text does it say that he was unbound! Perhaps he is not on the altar physically, but the psychic wounds are there for sure. He doesn't go back to Beersheba—in fact the midrash has him going to live with Hagar and Ishmael in Beer-lahai-roi. I can just see the three victims (Hagar, Ishmael and Isaac) commiserating together, wondering how Abraham was able to sacrifice all three of them. Does Ishmael still see himself as thrown behind the bushes, cast away with his mother in exile? He becomes an expert bowman (רבה קשת) but does not return to civilization, staying in the wilderness.

The three parents are both victims and perpetrators (perhaps Hagar less so than the other two). Can they make it up to their blameless children? And will their children be able to let go of their own traumas and be willing to forgive them? And should they?

I have always wondered why our sages have chosen these two texts for Rosh haShanah. Why start the year off with such problematic texts? Namely: child abuse, God's unreasonable demand of loyalty, kicking a child out of his home, enmity and jealousy between two women! All of these actions have lasting repercussions. Not only do they seem to be unforgivable, they are! Yet 'tis the season of *teshuvah*, when we are expected to make amends, to forgive and be forgiven. Each and everyone of us has to deal with our own past and decide how to deal with it. With all the problems that plague us, why are we obligated to read about the most dysfunctional family in history?

Perhaps the answer lies in that we are to understand that 'there but for the grace of God, go I'. We should learn how not to behave from the past. The problem is when we mix up the past and the present. If we excuse our ancestors' behaviour, and say this is what should be done, that stops us from dealing with the present rationally. If we demonise Hagar and Ishmael, because we see them as a threat to ourselves, and view Abraham of the bible as a *tsaddik*, we are committing an egregious travesty. If however, we demand of the Abrahams, Sarahs and Hagars among us to stop treating their children as objects, as pieces to be manipulated on the chess board, then we have the beginning of *teshuvah*.

During this season, we are in a time of constant readiness, to answer God's call (*hineni*). This puts a tremendous amount of pressure on us. The feeling is that when we start a new year, we can leave all of our troubles behind. But it is neither possible nor desirable to forget the past. There is no such thing as just ‘being in the moment’.

When I read about the planes unloading the 20,000 ecstatic worshippers of Rabbi Nachman of Breslov, one of the founders of the Jewish Hasidic movement. in the war zone of Uman, I shudder. Do they think God will protect them from Russian bombardments? Don’t they have any sense of history? Actually to me they have no sense at all.

They make me recall Abraham, who unthinkingly followed the directions of God on the path to Mt. Moriah. To do genuine *teshuvah*, and move forward, we have to look back first; we have to take full responsibility for the damage we have caused. But there are some things that cannot be fixed and that is the lasting damage done to the psyche of the children. PTSD is real. It means we cannot get away from our past. It is impossible to cleanse, to wipe out our memories, to reboot, as it were. It is unfair to demand of a victim that he forgive a perpetrator.

I will try to answer my question of why we read these stories on Rosh haShanah. If we consider the primacy of our relationship to God, rather than our relationship between ourselves, we are making a big mistake. And the proof of the pudding is that after these stories, God doesn’t speak to Abraham again, nor does Isaac, Ishmael, Hagar and Sarah. He is on his own completely. By choosing to worship and love God rather than defend and protect his two sons from the unreasonable demands of wife and God, he may have passed the test and proved to God that he loved Him, but he failed the real test—that of being a human being! In the past God may have demanded absolute loyalty and if you disobeyed, you were considered a sinner and punished.

But if we are absolutely loyal or totally committed to anything, including God, we are lesser beings, in that we are willing to sacrifice our sons/daughters to a cause. It is a mistake to call these people heroes, to see them as role models for ourselves or for future generations.

In a very important book *Arguing with God,* Anson Laytner, points out that when we argue with God, we are standing with God—and that is the true message of what God wants from us. We cannot demand of people with PTSD that they forgive and forget. At the most they can try and pick up the pieces—but if they cannot, no one is going to blame them. It would seem that of the Holy Triad, only Hagar succeeds. And perhaps that is why in the midrash, she is linked with Keturah, the new wife of Abraham [Genesis Rabbah 61:4].

She is the one who was able to use the divine message, save her son and move on. Perhaps this was the marriage that was meant to be—perhaps this was Abraham's doing teshuvah as well, to right the original wrong demanded by God.

The Creation Account of Genesis 1: Humanity as One Embroidery

David Frankel

Though Rosh haShanah is a day of central Jewish importance, it, in fact, represents the day of judgement for all human beings. This accords with the tradition that God created the first humans on Rosh haShanah [Leviticus Rabbah 29:1]. God, so to speak, reevaluates his creation of humanity, on the day that he made them, and we, as those created in God's image, similarly reevaluate our standing within God's world.

The story of the creation of the first humans is famously related in Genesis 1, where we read [verse 27], ויברא אלוהים את האדם בצלמו, בצלם אלוהים ברא אותו, זכר ונקבה ברא אותם, "Elohim created the human in his image, in the image of Elohim he created him, male and female he created them."

This verse has troubled exegetes from the time it was written. One problem, of course, was how to coincide what is stated here with the story of the creation of 'Adam' in Genesis 2:7. There, we are told that God created the first man from the dust of the ground. Woman is only created later, out of the rib of the man. Yet our verse seems to present man and women as created together, at the same time! The ancient biblical readers were troubled by another difficulty as well. The statement of

Gen 1:27 seems to be contradictory. At first it states that God created 'the man' in his image. Then it says that God created 'them' male and female. So did God create a single individual or a human couple?

One famous Midrashic solution suggests that God created the first human as a male and female, both attached in a single body [Bereshit Rabbah: 7—8]. It was thus a 'him' and a 'them' at the same time! The story of Genesis 2, accordingly, was not so much a removal of Adam's rib as a separation of the male-female unit into two individuals.

Modern scholarship, of course, takes a different approach. It finds in the beginning of Genesis two different creation accounts that did not agree in every detail. The creation account of Genesis 1 told of the creation of the human species in the form of a male and female couple. 'The man' that God created in his image, is thus a collective noun referring to the species – humanity. The word האדם is indeed used frequently as a collective noun, as in the striking divine statement made after smelling the pleasant aroma of Noah's sacrifice, "I will not continue to curse the earth because of humanity (האדם), because the willful heart of humanity (האדם) is evil from his youth..." [Gen 8:21].

There is thus no contradiction between the statement that God created humanity in God's image, and the further statement that God created humanity in the form of a plurality, that is, a male and a female. This is one coherent statement.

The story of Genesis 2, in contrast, presented God as first creating a man, then creating the animals, and finally creating a woman. Both stories speak of the creation of a first couple, but Genesis 1 presents the male and female as created at one time, and Genesis 2 presents them as created separately.

There is, however, another way of understanding the statement of Genesis 1:27, though very few interpreters have followed this approach. In this reading, what God creates is not a single human pair, as in the story of Genesis 2, but a full-on human community. The words "male and female he created them" are commonly interpreted as referring to a single male and single female because of the influence of the story of Genesis 2.

The more natural meaning of this phrase is that God created the first human community out of males and females. This parallels the reports of creation of the other creature types, which also seem to involve groups, referred to with collective nouns [cf. Gen 1:20, 22, 25]. Similarly, in many of the ancient Mesopotamian creation myths, humanity is created because the disgruntled lower gods refuse to continue labouring for the higher gods. The humans are thus created as a mass of labourers.

Following this interpretation, the difference between the two creation stories in Genesis is a profound one. Whereas the story of Genesis 2 presents the creation of an individual, the story of Genesis 1 presents the creation of a community of males and females. The Rabbis offered an important insight into the significance of the creation of humanity as an individual [Mishnah Sanhedrin 4:5]. The point, they said, was to remind us that every individual amounts to an entire world, and that each individual human being is infinitely sacred. What lessons can be derived from the presentation of humanity as created in the form of a community?

We must recall that according to Genesis 1:27, humanity is created in the image of God. This implies that the lone individual, sacred as he or she may be, is not a complete reflection of the divine. Something essential is missing. We fulfil our deepest essence as human beings, and live up to our commission to reflect the divine, when we ground our lives in the lives of the communities around us, and, ultimately, in the human community at large.

This means that we must promote harmony over divisiveness, cooperation over discord, and understanding over scorn. We live in a world of growing divisiveness, and the future of humanity at times seems bleak. On Rosh haShanah we recall that humanity was created as a harmonious community, and it is our highest responsibility to recreate it today.

Allow me to conclude by citing part of a song written by Motti Hammer, and sung by Chava Alberstein, "One Human Embroidery," **רקמה אנושית אחת:**

If we can learn how to soothe,
how to soothe the animosity,
if we can only learn.
If we can learn,
if we can learn how to quiet our rage,
despite our humiliation,
to ask forgiveness.
If we can learn to start from the beginning.
For all of us, yes all of us are a single,
living human embroidery.
If one of us departs from us,
something dies in us,
and something of us remains with him.

May we merit a year of understanding and harmony.

3

Aseret Y'mei Teshuvah

Teshuvah as Interpretation

Herzl Hefter

There are aspects of the Yamim Noraim which I have always found difficult. A dominant theme in the liturgy can be understood to be demeaning. We humans are portrayed as pathetic, sin filled and guilt ridden, compared to shards of clay, dust of the earth and the vanishing dream. Generally speaking, beating someone down is not a preferred or effective method to improve behaviour. So rather than dwelling upon the dismal stature of human beings, I have found an empowering narrative in the phenomenon of teshuvah.

The Talmud in Yoma 86b attributes the following to the sage Reish Lakish:

> Great is repentance, as one's intentional sins are counted for him as merits, as it is stated: "And when the wicked turns from his wickedness, and does that which is lawful and right, he shall live thereby" [Ezekiel 33:19], and all his deeds, even his transgressions, will become praiseworthy.

How are we to understand this enigmatic statement? I can more easily understand that repentance may induce forgiveness. How are we to understand, however, the total transfiguration of sinful deeds into meritorious acts?

The key lies in the power that human beings possess in the ability to interpret. Jews spend a great deal of time interpreting sacred texts and texts in general. But interpretation is much more than rendering new understandings through textual analysis. The thought of Friedrich Nietzsche can be helpful here.

> That the value of the world lies in our interpretation...that previous interpretations have been perspective valuations by virtue of which we can survive in life...that every elevation of man brings with it an overcoming of narrower interpretations; that every strengthening and increase of power opens up new perspectives and means believing in new horizons – this idea permeates my writings.
> [Nietzsche, *Will to Power* 616 (1885-1886)]

For Nietzsche, the Will to Power, the most fundamental human desire not only to survive but to thrive, is intimately bound to the ability we have to give meaning to our lives through our power to interpret and thereby construct our own realities. New interpretations mean new perspectives and new horizons. The power that interpretation exerts is not limited to fashioning a meaningful future; it has the potency to redefine the past. Nietzsche again:

> *Historia abscondita* – Every great human being exerts a retroactive force: for his sake, all of history is put on the scale again, and a thousand secrets of the past crawl out of their hiding places – into his sunshine. There is no telling what may yet become part of history.

> Maybe the past is still essentially undiscovered!
> So many retroactive forces are still needed!
> [Gay Science 34]

The 'retroactive force' which will reveal the 'hidden history' is the power we possess to interpret our past and give it the meaning that it needs to have in order to increase our mental well-being and vitality.

Rabbi Yitzchak Hutner, the famed Rosh Yeshiva of Chaim Berlin in New York, wrote to a student suffering from feelings of unworthiness and guilt reflecting the same idea. Citing the verse from [Mishlei 24:16]: "For a righteous man falleth seven times, and riseth up again", he interprets it to say that not despite his fall will he rise, but rather precisely because he falls he shall rise. This means that the religious failure, the sin, when it is properly leveraged should be understood as inextricably bound to the process of spiritual growth. This realisation frees the troubled soul of the burden and guilt over her past actions. The sin has been transformed through a new interpretation of the past.

Much has been written concerning the question of whether human beings possess free will to change their future. Teshuvah thus conceived is tremendously empowering, actually endowing us with the power to change the past through an act of Will. As individuals and collectives we carry the troubling and traumatic memories of the past. Our natural tendency is to repress those memories in order to continue. This rarely works.

Nothing can erase the empirical facts of what our deeds have begotten. Yet Reish Lakish calls upon us to confront our past and through an act of Will – *teshuvah* – find a way, an interpretation, which will confer a new meaning to our suffering which will engender vitality and thriving.

The Greatest Gift

Steven Gotlib

During the Yamim Nora'im, Jews around the world proclaim that *teshuvah* (repentance/fasting), *tefillah* (prayer), and *tzedakah* (charity) avert a negative decree from On High. The Artscroll Machzor, which many North American Orthodox or Traditional Jews use on those days comments that this proclamation is meant "to indicate that sincere repentance includes fasting, prayer recited in a loud voice, and donations to charity." That's all well and good, but it does little to explain how these three components of repentance are meant to relate to each other.

One suggestion may be that the three represent thought, speech, and action respectively. Teshuvah may be best embodied by the act of fasting, but is fundamentally about a shift in one's mentality. As Maimonides writes [Mishneh Torah Hilchot Teshuvah 2:2], "what constitutes *teshuvah*? A sinner should abandon their sins and remove them from their thoughts, resolving in their heart never to commit them again."

Tefillah is meant to be vocalised, as the Shulchan Arukh codifies [Orach Chayim 101:2]: "One should not merely think about the words of prayer in one's heart, but must actually pronounce the words and cause them to be heard in their own ears." Finally, *tzedakah* requires an unambiguous act of giving from oneself to another.

Within this framework, *teshuvah*, *tefillah*, and *tzedakah* might be seen not as three separate actions one can engage in to escape negative judgement but as three parts of a whole in which each builds on the other. Teshuvah is facilitated by being able to verbalise our desire to change and asking for what we need to do so via *tefillah*. Likewise, giving *tzedakah* is the act of (literally) putting our money where our mouth is and showing those prayers to be meaningful rather than empty words. The act of *tzedakah*, whether donating to particular people in need or to a valuable cause, might then be seen as the measurable fulfilment of all three.

In today's tumultuous times, the ability to give from ourselves to others must not be overlooked. Doing so not only constitutes a *tikkun* (repair) of what has been broken but may also put us in the shoes of Avraham Avinu, whose sense of *chesed* (kindness as expressed by giving to others) was instrumental to both beginning the Jewish people and encountering God within creation in the first place. In the words of a powerful *midrash* [Bereishit Rabbah 39:1]:

> "R. Isaac said: This [Gen. 12:1] can be compared to a person travelling from place to place, seeing a lit-up palace (*birah doleket*), and asking: "Is it possible that this palace could have no one to care for it?" The caretaker then appeared to him and said "I am the one who cares for this palace!" So too our father Avraham wondered "how could it be that this world has no caretaker?" Hashem then appeared to him and said, "I am the one who cares for this world!"

Thinkers like Rabbis Abraham Joshua Heschel, Jonathan Sacks, and Shai Held have noted that the phrase *birah doleket* can be interpreted either as lanterns being lit inside or as the palace being ablaze. If one understands it in the latter sense, a question must be asked: how can a palace on fire reveal God?

My personal suggestion is that God not revealing Godself to Avraham until after the latter questioned how it could be that no one was caring for the world burning around him is key to understanding the message. Asking the question rather than remaining indifferent or saying nothing shows concern and a willingness to act to put the fire out. Now that the concern has been, acknowledged, verbalised, and is ready to be acted on, God is ready to lend God's hand to Avraham in extinguishing the flames.

The same is true for us. Teshuvah allows us to realise what needs to change, *tefillah* allows us to articulate it, and *tzedakah* is the act of following-through. To be Jewish is not only to be intellectual or to pray piously, but to do our part to actively make the world tomorrow better than it was yesterday. As the Japanese art of Kintsugi teaches us, it sometimes takes gold to repair shattered pottery, but with proper care the end result can be more beautiful than the original.

An Exercise in Emotional Imagination

Jeremy Rosen

From the Bible onwards there has been a dichotomy between what in modern terms we can call the rational and the non-rational. The philosophical and the mystical. It has been one of the recurring themes in the work of the great Rabbi J.B. Soloveitchik that there is both tension as well as unity in the concept of God in relation to Halachah. And it is this duality, that runs through the thinking of Louis Jacobs *z"l*, which still influences the way I understand and experience the Yamim Noraim with the core phrase that Teshuvah, (repentance), Tefillah (prayer), and Tzedakah (charity) characterise the underlying theme of these days.

The Torah gives us this dual track through the two words that describe our relationship with God, אהבה Ahavah and יראה Yirah. I intensely dislike translations and definitions, useful as they may be. They are often betrayals (*Traduire Tradire Est*) not to say misleading. But these words are normally translated as 'love', and 'awe' or 'respect'. An emotional dimension and an intellectual or mental path. The relationship with God, although covenantal, is essentially a relationship of emotion – whether it is characterised as commitment or obedience.

The first principle of the Aseret haDibrot is not formulated as a law, that you must or must not believe in God, but rather a statement about the fundamental presence of God in the universe that we as individuals have to try to find a way of accepting, and interacting with, each in one's own way. To have a primary relationship that one commits to, which entails and parallels God's reciprocal commitment to us implied by a covenant, a Brit.

We have the supernatural commandments concerning God and other commandments relating to human beings and institutions. The written word provides the foundation upon which we need to add the emotion. But, what is often left out in theological discourse is this religious feeling, experience. You can command one to do something and test whether one is obeying or not, but there is no way of knowing if a person believes (although action certainly indicates one's commitment). But commands tend to dominate religious discourse – and we tend to be overawed by the plethora of commands.

The different categories are: ומשפטים תורות ומצוות חוקים Chukim, Mishpatim Mitzvot and Torot. But despite the differences, they all have two goals: 1) to strengthen the relationship between humans and God, and 2) between God and humans. בין אדם להשם ובין אדם לחבירו. When talking about the relationship with God the Torah constantly emphasises the human experience of love. Moreover, the Torah contains both poetry and prose – two different but parallel ways of communication in a written form.

We can approach these core words of the Yamim Noraim (Teshuvah, Tefillah, and Tzedakah), through a halachic, legal dimension which describes our obligations and defines our actions. But we can also access them through emotions.

Tefillah certainly is an experiential process that can inspire, comfort and function therapeutically. But it can also function behaviorally simply as an act and routine. Teshuvah is a word in the Torah used for God returning, being reconciled to the people after being alienated as much as humans to reconcile one with the other. Tzedakah is an affirmation of human concern for the other as well as a channel to reach God.

These are another example of the number three that recurs throughout the Torah: three versions of Biblical events, of the Sinai Revelation, the Tabernacle construction, so that the cord of three strands symbolises the unity of us, our traditions and God. These three words unite in the totality of the Jewish experience. The החוט המשולש. The rope of three strands that cannot easily be broken [Ecclesiastes 4:12].

All these three require us to use our imagination as a way of reinforcing the commitment through feeling, through a drama in which we are the actors. To imagine we are engaging with God, to imagine our life is an open book, and to face the challenge to do better, to achieve more through the mystical surrender that overcomes our rational reservations.

On Pesach we act as if we were slaves suddenly freed. On the Yamim Noraim, we have the sound of the *shofar*, which is designed to appeal to our senses and to bring us to repentance not through logic or rationality but through sounds, resonances, reminders. Then we act as if we are standing before a Divine Tribunal where everything – our errors, failures and omissions – are laid out before the Judge.

This exercise in emotional imagination, in acting *'as if'* triggers two conflicting emotions. The guilt on the one hand and the comfort we can derive from God's mercy and compassion. The balancing act between halachic obligation and encountering the passion of our relationship with God. The drama in other words of our relationship with other human beings and God through Halachah, action, and *devekut*, the mystical connection with the Divine.

R' Soloveitchik writes that "the message of repentance, which for Maimonides is implied in the sounding of the *shofar*, cannot serve as the cause of the commandment that would assure it a status of necessity, but it must be apprehended rather as an allusion to a correlated subjective aspect. *Kol shofar,* the sound of the shofar, only betokens self-examination and conversion. It merely indicates parallel tendencies in both subjective and objective orders".

A bridge between rationalism and mysticism.

Listening to Others so God Will Listen to Us

Francis Nataf

One of the most beautiful and inspiring illustrations of the power of prayer is told about King Hezekiah [Berachot 10]. Faced with a divine death sentence that Isaiah describes as irrevocable, Hezekiah chooses to ignore one of the greatest prophets of all time. Instead, he tells Isaiah that when it comes to prayer, even when the executioner's sword is upon our neck, there is no such thing as coming 'too late'. The Talmud endorses his position over that of Isaiah, telling us that Hezekiah's prayer was effective and pushed off the supposedly irrevocable decree.

This is presumably one of the sources for the cry uttered in so many congregations on the High Holy Days that prayer (along with repentance and charity) can remove a harsh divine decree.

Inspiring though it may be, it is difficult to relate to our own lives even on a good day, all the more so in times like ours. Moreover, it is theologically complicated by rabbinic statements that emphasise the attenuated relationship of God to the Jewish people after the destruction of the Temple. Such statements give us the sense that what was true for Hezekiah may not be entirely true today.

So where does that leave us, and where does it leave our prayers?

Practically speaking, we must recognise that the door to our prayers is still open, even if the opening is very small indeed. If anything, the difficulty of getting our prayers answered requires us to pray with even greater effort. When confronted by medical procedures that only have a small chance of saving a life, the importance of the goal makes most of us pursue it nevertheless. On some level, this was exactly Hezekiah's point. He was not saying that we would certainly be answered, nor even that there is a good chance we would be answered. Instead, his point was that prayer always has a chance of working, no matter how small.

But there is another problem. If our times are not the same as Hezekiah's, we are also not nearly the person Hezekiah was. Partly because of our ordinariness and partly because of the weakness of faith in our times, we cannot possibly compare ourselves to this spiritual giant. And it stands to reason that God will be likelier to listen to someone worth listening to. But that is not a binary proposition. There is certainly something we can do to make ourselves at least a little more worth listening to. Obviously, we cannot simply disregard God the whole year and then come crying to Him with all sorts of demands on Rosh haShanah.

Yet since there is so much to fix, where should we start? Perhaps God's poetic justice suggests that if we want God to listen to us even when He is not inclined to agree, perhaps we need to model that very behaviour toward others.

Some have suggested that we model ourselves on the respectful rivalry between Beit Hillel and Beit Shammai. Not only did that mean listening to one's opponents, it also meant granting them the legitimacy of their views. The Talmud [Yevamot 14a] famously tells us that they found ways to continue interacting in all areas while still being true to their own beliefs.

Yet such a comparison is easily dispelled. After all, these rival schools of thought had a great deal in common and were ultimately both engaged in the same esteemed pursuit at the same high level of scholarship. However, there is something even more fundamental missing from the comparison.

If we are trying to model what we want from God, we have to look at others the way God likely looks at us. If we want to continue to use Beit Hillel as the (albeit totally inadequate) metaphor for God, the metaphor for us (even after we try to improve ourselves) would need to be an immature, basically ignorant, highly inconsistent and uncouth (if often well-meaning) group of people. When we ask God to listen to our prayers, we are asking Him to listen to people who, from His lofty perspective, must not appear much different than those just described.

Are these not, after all, the terms we often use for our own opponents? More importantly, is this not the description we often use as an excuse for not listening to them? (I am not saying we always see our opponents in this light nor that it is justified when we do. I am simply presenting this as the worst, but all too common, scenario). If so, we would be well advised to internalise the divine wisdom that exists in God's nevertheless wanting to listen to those so inferior to Him.

Perhaps this is needed now more than ever. For though many of us remain focused on Israel's current war, the more general polarisation in Israeli society and throughout much of the world that preceded it and continues to serve as its backdrop should be an even greater concern. Polarisation turns a society from one that at least theoretically attempts to be win/win to one that operates exclusively by win/lose. As if you stand for the opposite of what I stand for, the only way to get my way is by defeating you.

Perhaps it is the holy spark that comes with being created in the image of God that makes all people worth listening to (if not necessarily acceding to their requests, just as God does not always accede to our requests). Or perhaps it is from the need to work on our humility that the Rabbis say exists wherever there is greatness (Moshe being only the most obvious example). Whatever the reason, however, if there is one thing we should work on this year, my vote is for truly listening to those with whom we disagree.

Teshuvah: A Springboard to Ascend to Closeness with the Divine

Yiscah Smith

"Return, O Yisrael, to the Eternal your God, for you have fallen because of your sin" [Hosea 14:2]

The Piaseczner asks:

> What kind of *teshuvah* is required of us. For when a person has remorse only for the sin that they stumbled on, whether it was committed, God forbid, in thought, in word, or in deed, they still find themselves back in the state they occupied before they committed the sin. In this case, the person has not yet become among those people more spiritually elevated and sensitive. Rather, they are now only relieved of their particular sin. The fundamental component of *teshuvah*, however, is "Return, O Yisrael, to the Eternal your God". Therefore, it is necessary to say this to you "...for you have fallen because of your sin," and lest you think that contrition for your sins alone is enough, therefore, the prophet cautions that the teshuvah must continue all the way, "until you reach the Eternal, your God". Only then will you be completely elevated in holiness, purity and being in service with the Divine. [Rabbi Kalonymus Kalmish Shapira]

We may view this radical teaching as the Piaseczner introducing a novel approach to 'doing *teshuvah*.' The magical and mystical dimension of *teshuvah* potentially results in the Jewish people now connecting to the Creator in a never-yet experienced way. A way where the integrity of our connection with the Divine is not only healed, at the very least, but even strengthened, bringing joy and cause for celebration.

In fact, I would argue that doing *teshuvah* 'only to be relieved of our particular sin' robs us of the infinite potential embedded in the spiritual practice of *teshuvah*. The process begins when we realise that our mistakes, *i.e.* sins, distance us from the Divine Presence dwelling within each of us. As if we become alienated from a deeper part of ourselves, feeling less connected to our inner being, our soul. The spiritual practice of *teshuvah* becomes our accepting the Eternal's invitation to move the needle — from sensing distance to cultivating closeness.

Through this lens, if we contemplate on our mistakes and learn from them, our *teshuvah* results in the capacity to ascend to a higher awareness of the Divine. This strengthens our connection and causes us to experience increased closeness to the Divine—more than our previous status quo allowed us.

Rabbi Schneur Zalman of Liadi writes:

> Every *yeridah* (descent) is for the sole purpose of a subsequent *aliyyah* (ascent). We may understand this as the trampoline effect: our

> sin results in our awareness of the Divine to be compromised — a descent of consciousness. Our *teshuvah*, from this lower place, now results in our springing up, ascending higher than where we were prior to our sin — "until you reach the Eternal, you God."

From the place of feeling far and distant from God, we are able to desire and seek closeness in a unique and even painful way. Hence, if we appreciate the power of *teshuvah* through the lens of the Piaseczner's understanding, we can catapult to an awareness of the Divine even more keenly than prior to our sin. For the Piaseczner, if our *teshuvah* merely brings us back to the spiritual place we experienced prior to committing the sin, we will have missed an incredibly unique opportunity to realise the full potential inherent in a sin.

In fact, I would suggest that as we cultivate our own unique spiritual practice of *teshuvah*, we consider diminishing our obsession over our errors and judging ourselves too harshly for our mistakes that have distanced us from God.

Admitting our wrongdoings is important because it is essential to assume responsibility for our part in the relationship with the Divine. But this begins the practice and does not complete it. Rather, might we begin to ask ourselves "what do I need to do differently to help me ascend to a higher awareness of the Divine that dwells within me so I can feel closer?"

Even further, the paradigm shift I am suggesting turns us away from excessively and externally focusing on 'doing it right' towards an internal experience of encountering the Divine in a more visceral and immanent way. To this end, my own sense is that we Jews—and humanity—are beginning to enter a new era of consciousness—a new zeitgeist. It brings with it a radical, redemptive and refreshing energy—along with unsurety, confusion and insecurity.

The concerns and questions that many people ask today, that gnaw at us, that we take to bed and wake up to and that influence our conversations with others are different than not that long ago.

What I increasingly hear within myself and from others, is the need for our *teshuvah* to bring us to an experience where we are connecting and sensing an encounter with the Divine, rather than checking off the boxes of 'doing teshuvah right'—which may meet external behavioural and legal expectations of us, but more often than not, leaves many of us feeling a bit empty and still far from the Divine—as if something is not right within us. We may have performed the ritual of *teshuvah* according to its halachic (Jewish legalistic) requirements but we may very well remain in the same spiritual place that caused us to sin to begin with.

Maybe this is the *teshuvah* that the still small voice within asks of us. A *teshuvah* that is valued as a practice to ascend "until you reach the Eternal, you God."

I Wait for God

Daniel Nevins

From the first sounding of the *shofar* on day one of Elul until the final dance circuit of Simchat Torah, the Days of Awe concentrate the mind. Over the course of these seven weeks, we probe perplexities and distil complex emotions until, ideally, they resolve into purpose, renewal, and joy. As the holidays of 5784 concluded, I felt close to attaining this spiritual climax, but it was violently shattered on the horrific Shabbat of Shemini Atzeret, October 7, 2024.

For many of us in the diaspora, the calamitous news from Israel arrived only as we entered synagogue to sing psalms of praise and remember our loved ones with the solemn prayers of *yizkor*. Suddenly, we plunged into emotional turmoil, absorbing with shock escalating estimates of the many Israelis killed or taken captive. Festive joy turned to sorrow, and the seven *hakafot* planned for that night gave way to a national experience of *shivah*.

As this dreadful year of war, worry and unmitigated loss proceeded, a type of clarity did emerge: *achdut*, the importance of Jewish unity.

Showing love for family and friends in Israel, opening our homes and institutions to visitors seeking shelter, marching in solidarity with the captives and their families, and flying to Israel on missions of comfort and support–these activities provided a fleeting sense of strength, of hope. But that surface solidarity could not mask our deep concern. The benign greeting of "how are you doing?" was often met with a shrug: "I am here". How do we regain our sense of confidence, of purpose, and joy?

I approach the 5785 Days of Awe seeking strength in our liturgy. This brings me to the haunting prayer, Ochilah la'Eil, 'I await God'.

This paragraph–a medley of verses from Psalms and Proverbs–appears on both Rosh haShanah and Yom Kippur in the reader's repetition of the Musaf service. It serves as a *reshut*, a poem in which the leader asks God's permission and guidance as they represent the congregation. This task is made explicit when the poet explains that they stand 'amidst the congregation,' (for this reason the poem is not said in the individual Amidah).

I am especially moved by the words taken from Proverbs 16:1. **לאדם מערכי לב, ומה' מענה לשון**, "Mortals may arrange their thoughts, but what they say depends on God." [JPS trans., 2023]. I understand this verse to mean that while a person struggles to organise their thoughts, the final expression, if coherent and true, comes from God. This is the experience of communal prayer with our poetic liturgy–not necessarily to understand the perplexities that trouble us, and not necessarily to transcend the sorrows that afflict us, but to become a channel for divine wisdom, forgiveness, and blessing.

A remarkable feature of this prayer is that it captures both the deeply personal and internal experience of organising one's thoughts before speaking, at the same time that it highlights the communal embeddedness of the speaker. Standing amidst the people, the leader of prayer finds their voice, their strength, and is able to address the Holy One.

The congregation strengthens the leader, and the leader elevates the righteousness of the congregation. This is true not only in leading prayer, but also when teaching Torah. At the end of his magnum opus, Beit Yosef [HM 426:2], Rabbi Yosef Karo uses the same expression, *ochilah la'eil*, to express hope that his halachic commentary will allow many Jews to grow in wisdom and righteousness, as indeed it has.

The Days of Awe are most effective when they stimulate us in both ways–our internal awakening, and our communal engagement. And while we all hope to achieve this state of exalted consciousness in moments of tranquillity, the truth is that the power of spiritual community is felt most acutely when facing misfortune.

On July 18, 2024, I stood in a mass memorial gathering in Buenos Aires, Argentina to mark the thirtieth anniversary of the bombing of the AMIA communal centre. My Spanish comprehension is nearly nil, and so the speeches sounded like doleful music. But then family members read the names of the 85 victims of that horrible act of terror for which no one has been held accountable, and I understood.

After each name was read, the crowd of many thousands cried out, "¡Presente!" I took this affirmation in two ways–that the dead are still present in our midst, and that we remain present to testify to their eternal value, to pursue justice on their behalf. From a state of confusion I entered a state of resolve, with the crowd causing my lips to respond. I became truly present.

As with the prayer Ochilah la'Eil, so too in moments of historical crisis, we may fail to express our thoughts and emotions alone. But in community, standing together, we can experience a divine voice emerging from our mouths, a voice of strength, wisdom and love, exceeding the capacities of our broken hearts. May the Holy One unite our hearts to pursue justice in 5785, and may God bless our people and the entire world with peace.

אוֹחִילָה לָאֵל. אֲחַלֶּה פָנָיו.
אֶשְׁאֲלָה מִמֶּנּוּ מַעֲנֵה לָשׁוֹן:
אֲשֶׁר בִּקְהַל עָם אָשִׁירָה עֻזּוֹ.
אַבִּיעָה רְנָנוֹת בְּעַד מִפְעָלָיו:
לְאָדָם מַעַרְכֵי לֵב. וּמֵיְהֹוָה מַעֲנֵה לָשׁוֹן:
אֲדֹנָי, שְׂפָתַי תִּפְתָּח. וּפִי יַגִּיד תְּהִלָּתֶךָ:
יִהְיוּ לְרָצוֹן אִמְרֵי פִי וְהֶגְיוֹן לִבִּי לְפָנֶיךָ יְהֹוָה צוּרִי וְגוֹאֲלִי:

4

Yom Kippur

The Origin of Teshuvah

Deborah Kahn-Harris

The word that we translate as 'repentance' does not appear in the Tanakh – a fact that may be surprising to many. To be sure the Hebrew word, *teshuvah*, which we normally translate as 'repentance', does appear in the Tanakh, where it means either 'return' [I S 7:17; II S 11:1; & I Chr 20:1] or 'reply' [Jb 21:34]. But the earliest sources where we might identify *teshuvah* as meaning anything at all similar to the concept we now refer to as 'repentance' is probably from the Damascus Document, a text of the post-biblical Qumran community [CD 19:16].

The word *teshuvah* is from a Hebrew root that fundamentally relates to the concept of 'return, go back' in a largely literal sense. Abraham went somewhere and then 'returned' to the place from whence he started out [cf., Gen 18:33]. So how did this rather mundane word transform from its baseline meaning in Biblical Hebrew to the spiritual concept we generally understand it to mean today? If 'repentance' is not, after all, biblical, what is happening in all of those prophetic texts where the People of Israel are enjoined to 'return to God'? What pitfalls might we find in our evolved understanding of *teshuvah*? What might that mean for us as we begin to reflect on the famous rejoinder of our penitential liturgy that 'repentance, prayer, and charity avert the harsh decree'?

In his foundational work on the subject, *How Repentance Became Biblical: Judaism, Christianity, & The Interpretation of Scripture*, David A. Lambert traces precisely this history. He discusses how later generations have read 'repentance' back into the Tanakh employing what he terms 'the penitential lens' [David A. Lambert 2015 *How Repentance Became Biblical: Judaism, Christianity, & The Interpretation of Scripture*, OUP:NYC,3].

He employs a number of interpretative strategies that in turn are based on certain assumptive principles. In particular, I want to focus briefly on one of those assumptions, namely that of interiority. Lambert defines interiority as the notion that 'we have "outsides" and "insides" with our essence located in the latter' [Lambert, 5].

For many of us this assumption of interiority is so basic as to be essentially hidden from us. What are we doing when we repent – particularly through *tefillah*, prayer – if we are not internally scrutinising ourselves, seeking some sort of reconstruction of our own psychological makeup and deeply internalised, personal behaviours?

In the biblical world, 'returning to God' involved a range of largely external behaviours – sacrifices, fasting, public displays of mourning rituals. These activities were designed predominately to placate an angry God, thus, addressing the breakdown of the Divine-human (particularly Israelite) covenantal relationship.

But when we turn only towards our own subjective internal experience, we run the risk both of alienating ourselves from the communal space as well as relegating the external world to something merely superficial. In a biblical framework that community framework is foundational, albeit too often problematically heteropatriarchal in construction. So what of the world beyond our own interior discourse? Does the materiality of the external world not profoundly impact our experiences and behaviours?

Lambert writes by way of warning that:

> "[t]he privileging of interiority commits us to a hermeneutic of absence, to looking at all material representations as merely surface phenomena expressing some more essential reality. Such a hermeneutic allows manifestations of difference to be subsumed, colonised...by our universal categories." [Lambert, 191]

Perhaps, then, part of the answer lies not so much in the need to reconstruct and, thus, return us to the biblical origins of meaning *teshuvah* and its root, as it is to reincorporate some of this origin story this term into our own theology of repentance. How would thinking of *teshuvah* beyond only an internal monologue potentially enhance our theology, rituals, and practices? How could we represent both the exteriority and interiority of what is currently embodied in the act of *teshuvah*?

In this brief reflection, I seek merely to ask the questions, not yet to answer them. I hope to stimulate consideration of the world beyond our own interiority which, certainly across much of the Western, democratic world, has shaped so much of a sense of selfhood. And given how many of us, particularly those who all too often only attend during the Yamim Noraim, are present in the communal space of congregational life on Rosh haShanah and Yom Kippur, I wonder what more we could all gain from considering the practice of *teshuvah* as truly rooted in both the interior and exterior worlds we inhabit.

Fleeing from God

Louis Jacobs, z"l

> "But Jonah rose up to flee unto Tarshish from the presence of the Lord . . ." [Jonah I, 3]

Jonah, the prophet of the Lord, knew, remarks the Midrash, that God is everywhere, that you cannot fly from Him in space. What then was the purpose of the prophet's flight to Tarshish? Jonah had been taught, answers the Midrash, that the Divine Presence can rest on the prophet only in the Holy Land, so that by escaping to a land where holiness was unknown, by deliberately submitting to an inferior way of life and thus forfeiting the right to see the prophetic vision, he thought to evade the tremendous responsibility that is part of the prophet's burden.

The illustration is given of the slave of a priest who runs from his master into a graveyard, knowing that the priest is forbidden to enter the place of death and contamination. But the master says: Foolish slave! I cannot come into the graveyard but I have other slaves whom I can send there to bring you back to me."

How true to life this is! Do we not try to escape God's presence? Do we not try to shirk our responsibilities? Do we not, at times, throw ourselves into a feverish round of activities—some of them even worthwhile activities—in order to still our consciences? Do we not, on occasion, deliberately choose an inferior way of life in the knowledge that its demands on our time, our thought, our energies, will be less severe?

It is not an easy thing to live in the presence of God. As a modern religious poet puts it:

Forgive us, O Lord, we acknowledge
ourselves as type of the common man.
Of the men and women
who shut the door and sit by the fire,
Who fear the blessing of God,
the loneliness of the night of God,
the surrender required,
the deprivation inflicted,
Who fear the injustice of men
less than the justice of God.

The story is told of a famous Russian rabbi who, one Kol Nidrei eve, after the service in the synagogue, noticed a wealthy man with a niggardly reputation, sitting reciting psalms with the evident intention of spending the night in this way. Whereupon the rabbi went up to him and said: "My good man, you are a deserter." "A deserter, rabbi! What do you mean?" "It is quite simple," the rabbi replied. "In an army there are many kinds of soldiers: infantry, cavalry, engineers, and so on. Now supposing an infantryman decided, in the heat of the battle, to join the ranks of the cavalry, would he not be a deserter?

The recitation of Psalms after Kol Nidrei is a good occupation for poor scholars. But you have been called to a different role in life. It is your duty to go home and have a good night's sleep, but to resolve in the future to be more liberal with your wealth."

The trouble with attempting to fly from God is that it just does not work. We may throw ourselves with zest and enthusiasm into the form of escapism we have chosen, but sooner or later we recall nostalgically that to tread the path of duty had its beauties as well as its severities, its privileges as well as its demands.

Yom Kippur, with its haunting melodies and colourful ritual, its inspiring services and its reminder that we belong to a great people with a glorious history of seeking and finding God, is one of the ways He uses to awaken within us the sense of loyalty to our faith and our people so that we repeat with deep emotion the words of the Prophet: "I will go and return, for then was it better with me than now."

Unetaneh Tokef and Human Flourishing

Harris Bor

"Who by water, who by fire..." - It's hard to imagine how a prayer about judgement and death could be so inspiring, but Unetaneh Tokef hits the mark every time. The tune no doubt plays a part, but it also gets at the core of the religious instinct; our mortality, our longing for the infinite, awe. We are but 'a passing shadow... a vanishing cloud.' Our only hope is to cling to the 'King who lives eternal.'

Our sense of vulnerability needs no coaxing this year. Fear is everywhere: terror, war, hatred, political turmoil, climate change, the encroachment of technology. Yet, we are not entirely hopeless.

After listing all the ways we might die, Unetaneh Tokef tells us that 'repentance, prayer, and righteousness lessen (*ma'avirin*) the severity of the divine decree.' Note, these things do not divert or remove the divine decree. They only lessen its impact. In other words, they can't bring out the sunshine, only help us weather the storm.

This is a departure from the Talmudic and Midrashic sources for this prayer, which take a different theological approach. A Talmud passage citing Rabbi Yitzchak, tells us that charity, crying out, changing one's name, and altering one's actions 'rip up' a person's sentence [Talmud Bavli Rosh haShanah 16b]. A Midrash similarly records Rabbi Yudin stating, in the name of Rabbi Eliezer, that repentance, prayer, and righteousness 'nullify evil decrees' [Bereishit Rabbah 44:12]. There is no mere weakening of the divine decree here.

Maimonides marks a possible change of focus. He codified the four paths from the Talmud as 'among the ways of repentance' but is careful not to link them to any external change in circumstance [MT, Hilchot Teshuvah 2:4].

Kalonymus (d. 1096), the liturgical poet who is said to have been taught Unetaneh Tokef in a dream, appears to adopt the Midrashic formula, but to place it into a theological context somewhere between Maimonides and the Talmud.

Contra Maimonides, the paths of repentance, prayer, and righteousness have an impact. But the effect is not to remove evil (as in the Talmud and Midrash) but to make life more tolerable. This I think better reflects our phenomenological experience than the Talmud or Midrash.

We might also give the prayer a more positive spin. Repentance, prayer, and righteousness are not just about mitigating the bad, but allowing us to flourish in every aspect of our being.

In the science of education and holistic and transformative learning, it is common to refer to the development of the heart, head, and hand.

The head symbolises intellectual engagement. The hand represents our direct involvement with the world, artistry, and practical skills. The heart is our emotional attachment to the things we learn and the world.

All these aspects are involved in learning and require to be cultivated. The development of emotion through learning includes love, faith, beauty, trust, gratitude, and aesthetics. Only when we have strong feelings about what we learn do we give significance to it. Physical movement and dexterity have a close connection to learning and are key aspects of production and artistry.

We can map the aspects of head, heart, and hand on the paths of repentance, prayer, and righteousness. The first step of repentance is acknowledging our mistakes. For Maimonides, we repent by removing sins from our thoughts, expressing remorse (Vidui), and resolving not to repeat our errors [MT, Hilchot Teshuvah 2:4]. There is a strong intellectual component to this exercise. It begins with the head.

Prayer of course is about opening our hearts. The last prayer of the Yom Kippur service is called Neilah (the locking), commonly thought to be a reference to the locking of the gates of repentance. However, a midrash cited in R' Bachya Ben Asher's *Kad ha-Kemach* (14th C) suggests that the gate being locked is not of repentance but our hearts. This is the only gate for which God doesn't have the key. Like the lover in the Song of Songs [5:5], at Neilah God knocks at the gates of our hearts and asks to be let in.

Righteousness (Tzedakah) is primarily about the physical act of charity, the work of the hand. The highest form of charity is to grant someone a gift or loan or to join her in partnership, or to find him work [Shulchan Aruch, YD 249:6; MT, Gifts to the Poor, 10:7].

More fundamentally, we might relate these three paths of repentance, prayer, and righteousness to the call in the Shema to love God with all our heart (*lev*), with all our soul (*nefesh*) (intellect or head) and with all our possessions (*meod*) (hand) [Devarim 6:5].

As indicated, prayer corresponds to heart, repentance to head, and charity to hand. The presence of these three aspects of head, heart, and hand in the Shema signals their centrality to Jewish practice.

Our ultimate task, therefore, is not to cower before the divine to avoid punishment but to fulfil ourselves fully as human beings in relationship with the divine.

Broken, but Beautiful

Adam Zagoria-Moffet

It all began by breaking.

At least that is, according to Rabbi Isaac Luria's understanding of how the universe was made. In the 16th century, Luria put forward a new mythology of creation – one centred on creativity, but also on cataclysm.

Before anything came into being, when the universe was chaos and void, the only thing that existed was a pure, undifferentiated, infinite Light. It was in every place possible, because at that time there was no such thing as 'place'. In every direction, to every degree, there was the Infinite Light. In order to begin the process which we call 'creation,' the Light had to recede from a particular spot, creating a 'place,' a vacuum empty of anything, for the only 'thing' was the Light.

Held back at the edges of this void, the Light meant to assemble a universe inside the vacuum– but if it simply filled it back in, everything would again be overwhelmed with pure undifferentiated Light.

Instead the Light created something to hold the space. It formed vessels of material reality – the containers which were meant to hold the world. Once the containers were in place, the Light trickled back in, very very slowly – so as not to overwhelm this new reality. However, even this slow flow of Light was too much, and the vessels shattered like crystal, dispersing into innumerable pieces. This catastrophic destruction couldn't be reversed, so instead the Light attempted to form a universe inside the void a second time– except this time the trickle of Light into the vessels was barely anything – a hairsbreadth compared to the width of the entire universe. Yet, in this smaller quantity, the system was stabilised.

The light poured back into the void, now structured as a world, and in that new world it took on many different forms – creating all material and spiritual reality, infusing itself into everything that lives – from galaxies and nebulae to dust mites and mitochondria.

Thus, the universe, our universe – is a second try. The cosmic collapse which characterised the first go at it resulted in fragments of the original vessels scattered throughout the universe; embedded in all things, waiting to be discovered, gathered, recombined, and reunited.

This myth of Creation may sound like the motifs of a pop-science programme, but Luria's conception of Creation was informed by his readings of Jewish mystical and philosophical sources, as well as his own innovation – and it has become incredibly influential on your life– even if you don't know anything about it.

Luria called this myth, *shevirat hakelim* (the shattering of the vessels) and it provided a basis for his entire worldview – one in which God is an Infinite Light equally present in all living organisms and one in which we bear the partial responsibility to help find, collect, and repair the shards of that first attempt at creation which are in the world all around us, and within ourselves.

Luria referred to this process of repairing the original cosmic scaffolding as various things– when discussing how it related to personal character development it was *tikkun atzmut* (self-repair) and when relating it to a broader goal it was nothing less than *tikkun olam* (world-repair).

These days, *tikkun olam* has become a fashionable by-word for social justice, and not without some basis. However, as the myth above suggests, it is a lot more than that – and it is not only exterior but interior as well; repairing the world and repairing ourselves are one in the same thing, since at root the Light is equally present in each of us as it is in all other forms of life.

The narrower sense of this concept, what Luria calls *tikkun atzmut* (self-repair) is something for which he found ample texts to use as a basis – including two which we recite during the High Holy Days – *unetaneh tokef* and *ki hineh kachomer*.

Our liturgy is flush with imagistic ways of trying to get our attention. Particularly on the High Holy Days, the *machzor* utilises so much poetry and literary flourish that, actually, much of it is lost on us in the torrent of prayers which we recite. Yet in and amongst all those words there are discrete themes, and one of them is about human fragility – what it means to be broken and what it means to be fixed. Three times in ten days we recite Unetaneh Tokef, and in it, a series of poetic analogies attempting to describe the course of human life:

> Each person's origin is dust, and each person will return to the Earth having spent life seeking sustenance. Scripture compares mortals to: broken pottery, withering grass, a shrivelled flower, a passing shadow, a fading cloud, a fleeting breeze, scattered dust, and a vanishing dream.

All of these beautiful images are drawn from the Tanakh, and all describe elements of the strictly natural world, except one: mortals are compared to broken pottery. That's the line that stands out to me and, especially in light of Isaac Luria's vision of creation, I think it is an appropriate intention for us to set for the holiest day of the year.

Of that list, pottery is the only thing which is made. Taking sediment from the Earth to make clay, it is shaped by heat and pressure and centripetal force into something usable – a vessel, a container, a material which can be filled and emptied, which when overfull, overflows and when it falls – it breaks.

That is precisely the image which Luria's doctrine of *shevirat hakelim* aims to leave us with. The question, of course, is what do we do with the fact that our universe is best understood as suffused with broken fragments of earthenware. To answer that, we have to look at another place where the theme appears – a *piyyut* which we sing only on Kol Nidrei, *ki hineh kahomer.*

The poem relies on several successive images relating to artisanal crafts: we are like clay in the hand of the potter, we are like stone in the hand of the mason, we are like iron in the hand of the blacksmith, we are like the helm in the hand of a sailor, we are like glass in the hand of the glazier, we are like cloth in the hand of the draper, we are like silver in the hand of the smelter. All of these try to get us to think of ourselves as material – something to be worked, developed, twisted, shaped, melted, thickened or thinned, preserved or broken.

Emphasising our vulnerability, these passages beautifully illustrate the idea of broken vessels – but the question remains, what do we do?

Luria suggested that the course of life is one in which we are meant to gather up these dispersed pieces of broken worlds and reassemble them. Some we may find in our own souls, some in the world around us. But, I think that there's another lesson here that our tradition never states, but that we can learn from other sources.

Japanese culture is renowned for its crafts, and there's two which make our point well – *sashiko* and *kintsugi.* Sashiko is a technique for repairing cloth. Typically done when cloth became threadbare and needed to be patched, *sashiko* is a method of applying a patch – but quite different from what we might immediately suspect. Most of us, if asked to patch something, would aim to conceal, as much as possible, the fact that it was ever repaired. We try to disguise the patch– with the sign of success being that someone couldn't tell it was ever torn in the first place. Sashiko does this differently – it emphasises the repair.

Using indigo cloth and white cotton thread, sashiko involved patching clothing with beautiful geometric patterns that achieve two aims: 1) to show that it has obviously been repaired, and 2) to use the opportunity to repair as a way to strengthen the original fabric. By using small geometric stitches and not knotting the thread, *sashiko* makes the fabric which it fixes stronger, more flexible, and more beautiful than it ever was before it was broken.

Similarly, and more to our point, we should consider the art of *kintsugi*. Kintsugi is a method of repairing broken pottery which takes the glue used to hold it together again and mixes it with gold. The result is a repaired vessel where the original cracks are emphasised, not hidden. Not only are the breakages visible, but they are made beautiful through the gold.

The underlying philosophy is the same as *sashiko* – that something which has been damaged and repaired is better for the repair, not worse because of it. Not only do these arts celebrate repair, they beautify it. To see a ceramic vessel laced through with golden glue where it had previously broken illustrates a lesson we can apply well to Luria's theology and our *machzor's* themes – broken is beautiful. Fixing something is not an effort to pretend it never broke in the first place, but to showcase how much stronger it can be after having been invested with work, effort, time, and love in putting it back together. Torn clothing adorned with *sashiko* patterns and broken vessels beautified with *kintsugi* golden fault lines can tell us how we are to repair ourselves and the world.

If we accept the ideas of Isaac Luria, that we and the world are full of broken pieces of a prior creation, then we should also apply the Japanese philosophy behind *sashiko* and *kintsugi* to it. In our repair, of our souls and our world, we are making things beautiful.

If we are broken – it is not that we are meant to restore things to how they were before. Rather, we should embrace the broken shards all around us and in fixing them, emphasise the fact of their repair. The vulnerability engendered by being compared to broken pottery, by comparing ourselves to cloth in the hand of the draper – that exact vulnerability is our strength, not our weakness.

We have work to do. Yom Kippur is the zenith of our annual efforts to put ourselves back together. If we engage honestly and openly with the process of *teshuvah* then we can fix a great deal – but we mustn't try and hide the work of *tikkun atzmut* or *tikkun olam*.

We must beautify it, showcase it, adorn it with beautiful patterns and golden glue. The work that we do today, and every day, shouldn't hide the cracks and fissures of those first broken vessels, it should celebrate them.

Being broken and repaired is not a failure, or a catastrophe, but an opportunity to become stronger, better, and more beautiful.

One of the many sayings of R' Nachman of Breslov was this: if you believe that it is possible to be broken, then believe that it is possible to be fixed. This Yom Kippur, may we all believe that the fixing we do is more than just restoring things to how they were. May we take the opportunity to fix ourselves, to fix the world – to make it better and stronger.

Mortals may be compared to broken pottery – but it is up to us whether that pottery remains the shattered remnants trapped in reality, or whether it becomes a beautiful new vessel, reconstructed with love, with hard work, and celebrating the cracks and fissures which shine from it in a new golden hue.

Jonah and the Reluctance of Religious Dogma

Simon Eder

A Universal Story

Bernard Henri-Levy, the renowned French philosopher makes a compelling case for the universalism of the Book of Jonah. Jonah is of course one of the few prophets commanded to save those of non-Hebrew origin and to deliver the prophetic warning to the great city of Nineveh, despite the fact that its inhabitants number 'more than 120,000 persons who do not know the difference between their right and left hand, as well as many animals'[1] To Levy, what God is signalling to Jonah is the importance of the city. As he expressed in an interview whilst discussing his book, *The Genius of Judaism* - "A city may be bad, but this way of creating community with the world that is what we call a City is a school for liberty that we cannot let be extinguished."[2]

Certainly one of Jonah's central tenets that God's mercy is found beyond sectarian divisions (Jonah's main reluctance to obey his summons is that he is concerned that Nineveh, the capital city of Assyria's repentance will be to the detriment of the prophet's own people as they are such sworn enemies) would give credence to Levy's argument. The text is also at pains to emphasise the dignified and admirable behaviour of those non-Hebrews and indeed of their recognition of the Lord. The sailors, for example, despite Jonah's plea that they should throw him overboard, cry out:

> 'Oh, please, Lord, do not hold us guilty of killing an innocent person! For You, Oh Lord, by your will have brought this about.'[3]

Levy shares a powerful story of how he came to resonate with the Book of Jonah. Back in August 2011 he was visiting Libya on behalf of the French government and found himself face-to-face with three well-known jihadists. He even spent a full night discussing important political and intellectual topics. What on earth had impelled him to meet with such avowed antisemites?

Leaving the armed camp the following morning he turned to one of the books that he had with him that contained a volume of the Book of Jonah, which provided the spark for a realisation that his own journey to Benghazi could indeed be likened to rescuing Nineveh. This in turn provided something of an impetus for his own deeper enquiry into his Jewish roots.

Levy's pointedly secular 'affirmative Judaism' of actions, not faith, ethics, not belief as well as the universalistic message that he draws from the text are however not the only way to frame the story. In fact it's themes of following God's will, repentance and prayer conform to traditional notions of Jewish thinking and practice.

Jonah's Date with Destiny

Like other prophets, Jonah exhibits significant reluctance to carry out his mission. Moses, no less, expressed his own resistance to undertaking the task that God had set him at the burning bush. Several times in the opening chapter the text uses the verb yarad 'to go down' indicating Jonah's Divine defiance. It is of course after his journey on board the boat initially in the very opposite direction to where he had been told to go, the storm and then his three day sojourn inside the giant fish that he finally comes to realise that a flight from God is indeed impossible.

It is in a somewhat parallel vein that I am reminded of the story of the treasure under the bridge:

> Once a Jewish inhabitant of Austria saw in his dream that under a bridge in the city of Vienna a valuable treasure lay buried. He journeyed there, stood on the bridge and wondered what to do, as it was impossible to search by day in case people saw him searching and realised that there was something going on. By the by, a soldier crossed the bridge, saw the Jew standing and wondering, and asked him:
>
> 'What are you doing here and what are you looking for?'
>
> The Jew thought about it, and told his secret to the soldier, asking him to help him search for the treasure so that they might share it 50/50

when they found it.

But the soldier replied: 'I feel sorry for you, you crazy dreamer! I also dreamed that a valuable treasure lay buried in the cellar of such and such a Jew in such and such a town, but am I going to set off on a journey there?!'

The name of the Jew was this man's name, and the town he had named was his hometown!

Whereupon the Jew took a wagon hitched to two sturdy horses and hastened to journey to his town, went down to his cellar, and there discovered the treasure.

At the sight of it, the Jew declared:

'Now this mystery has been revealed to me. The treasure had always lain buried in my house, but I had to leave my town and wander far far away to Vienna in order there to discover it in my house.'[4]

Of course in Jonah's case it is not treasure in question but the very word of God and he seeks flight from his calling rather than the pursuit of it. Nonetheless both stories exhibit a symmetry. In the book of Jonah this is the mirroring of the opening of chapters 1 and 3 which both feature God's instruction to Jonah. Just as the treasure features at the beginning and end prior to the intervening journey so is God's repeated injunction to Jonah with the whirlwind of his journey in-between.

One Midrashic interpretation has Jonah represent the people of Israel since Israel is compared to a dove, the very Hebrew meaning of the name Jonah. Its emphasis is then that the Jewish people can never escape its destiny as the people who proclaim the unity of God.[5]

Jonah's eventual acceptance of his divine duty and resolution within his conflicted soul, demonstrating an example of what William James termed 'the unity of the self' is also illustrative of the process of teshuvah, which is such a prominent theme within the book.

Teshuvah in the Book of Jonah

The readiness of the Ninevites to turn their back on their evil ways, making their embrace of repentance the most supreme example in all biblical literature (it is certainly the fastest and all-encompassing of any group) is the simplest example of teshuvah in the book. Strikingly Jonah's 5 Hebrew words 'Forty days more, and Nineveh shall be overthrown!'[6] is enough to prompt collective fasting and a series of penitential rituals all resulting in God's abandonment of His intention to destroy the city.

It is Jonah's teshuvah too which occupies much of the narrative. In many ways it conforms to Maimonides' principles of teshuvah namely regret, rejection and finally resolution.

Regret is perhaps the most difficult step in repentance because of the infinite human capacity for inertial evil and self-justification. We see this step when Jonah first acknowledges to the sailors that 'the terrible storm came upon you on my account'.[7] Jonah's fessing up and imploring of the sailors to throw him overboard marks the beginning of his awakening to his misdeed.

The second step in Jonah's journey of teshuvah, sparked by heartfelt prayer in the depths of despair whilst inside the belly of the giant fish is his rejection of wrong-doing, rejection of the futile path that he has chosen against the divine will that had caused such turmoil, a rejection of a course of action in which he had spurned God's call.

The final stage in Jonah's transformative process is then resolution:

> 'What I have vowed I will perform'[8]

It is this which then leads to his salvation and deliverance from the fish's belly onto dry land. There is however one final confirmatory step which also forms the ultimate proof of transformation in Maimonides' codification also exhibited by Jonah. This is that when confronted by a similar situation with the opportunity to commit sin, the correct path is taken. It is then on hearing God's second call to urge Nineveh on its path to repentance and to which Jonah adheres that we can then agree that his own *teshuvah* is complete.

Tefillah in the Belly of the Giant Fish

Perhaps the most moving lines of the story, which some scholars argue are later additions to the text, are those lines of poetry placed in Jonah's mouth, revealing his tormented soul and desperate for God's mercy.

Inside the belly of the fish, Jonah, deprived of any possible occupation or distraction (rather like the day of Yom Kippur) opts for the examined life. His descent into death then has the somewhat paradoxical result in re-energising his life forces and he recalls those scenes so dear to him of God's Temple. With life quite literally suspended for him as he turns ever inward seeking salvation through his prayer, he finds rebirth and renewal.

It is also through his prayer that we come to understand his dialectic between despair and faith. Quite literally at the bottom of the ocean, within the narrow confines of the belly of a fish, with nowhere left to hide, he finds his maker: "The bars of the earth closed upon me forever, yet you brought my life up from the pit"[9]

Indeed Jonah's very despair becomes a source of faith in his capacity to work at his inner transformation. From despair, to thanksgiving and ultimately to deliverance, Jonah's prayer is the very template for all who have reached rock bottom.

Jonah and The Reluctance of Religious Dogma

The book then manifests many traditional themes - the divine call, repentance, prayer and yet they all have something of a radical twist.

The book is certainly no manual for following God's instructions. Were that the case the whole story would commence in chapter 3. Indeed it is in Jonah's defiance of the original divine command that he finds the greatest opportunity for personal growth. So it is with us as we face our own challenges, perhaps veering from a safer path that we too find the greatest opportunity for growth and through mistakes, sometimes maybe even deliberate ones we may reach ever greater heights in the long run.

The book is often championed as demonstrating God's concern for all. Indeed it is the only biblical book ending with a question. Its question in fact is something of a reprimand to Jonah in his questioning of God's mercy for the people of Nineveh. And yet perhaps, Jonah, who in the end does not lose his argumentative nature with God does have a point. The Ninevites repentance as we explored might have been quick but unlike Jonah's own arduous transformation, theirs lacks inner work. In one Midrashic comment, the people of Nineveh after their forty days reverted to their wicked ways and God does eventually destroy the city. On this, Rabbi Jacobs commented that this line is so at variance with the story itself that it seems to have been pursued in defence of the Jewish people.[10]

The Ninevites repentance however was so heavily caught up in external trappings that perhaps the midrash is closer to the mark than Rabbi Jacobs gives credence.

Perhaps the most important hallmark of the book is in fact the signature trait that Jonah exhibits throughout, of his continued wrestling with God. In this of course he is in good company with those founding fathers of our tradition including Moses, Jacob and Abraham no less!

We can therefore agree with a central thrust of Levy's own book that the genius of Judaism is:

> "The absolute reluctance at any dogma, frozen thoughts, admitted truth [that is] not fake. It gives to no one person to own the formula of the perfect community in front of which each human should kneel down and accept and revere."[11]

It is this spirit which Jonah emulates and to which we would do well to emulate too.

[1] Jonah 4:11
[2] Tom Teichelz, Interview with Bernard Henri-Levy, *Forbes*, 25th January 2017
[3] Jonah 1:14
[4] Rabbi Nachman of Breslov, *Rabbi Nachman's Stories*, Breslov, p.478
[5] Jacobs, *The Jewish Religion; A Companion*, p.288
[6] Jonah 3:4
[7] Jonah 1:12
[8] Jonah 2:10
[9] Jonah 2:7
[10] Jacobs, *The Jewish Religion; A Companion*, p.288
[11] Tom Teichelz, Interview with Bernard Henri-Levy, *Forbes*, 25th January 2017

The Gates Never Close

Benjamin Elton

The most remarkable aspect of Yom Kippur is not that it is long, but that it is short. It moves very fast, so how should we most productively use it?

I want to answer that question from an unlikely starting point, from the example of someone who was told not to return, not to repent, not to repair his relationship with God. It is the case of Elisha ben Abuya, the Sage who became a heretic, and who is often called Acher, meaning simply 'the other one'. Elisha was the teacher of the great Rabbi Meir, who kept in touch with his old master even after Elisha abandoned Judaism.

Once Rabbi Meir was teaching in his Beit Midrash on Shabbat when his followers came to tell him that Elisha was riding past on his horse. Rabbi Meir went to greet him, and walked alongside the horse as the two discussed Torah. Rabbi Meir could not let go of Elisha just as Elisha could not let go of the Torah. They had been walking for a while when Elisha changed the subject of their conversation. The Talmud tells us what happened next:

> Elisha said to him, this is enough, Meir, this is the extent of the Shabbat boundary. [You are not allowed to walk any further]. Rabbi Meir asked him, how do you know? Elisha told him, from the horse's hooves which I continuously counted for two thousand cubits.

> Rabbi Meir said to Elisha, all that wisdom is in you and you do not repent? He told him, I cannot. Rabbi Meir asked him, why? Elisha told him, once I was passing by the Holy of Holies riding on a horse on the Yom Kippur which fell on Shabbat and I heard an Heavenly voice coming from the Holy of Holies, saying, '*shuvu banim shovavim chutz mi-Elisha ben Abuya*' – 'return, erring children, except for Elisha ben Abuya, who knew My power and rebelled against Me'.

Elisha ben Abuya was filled with Torah and wanted to carry on learning Torah, and deep down wanted to return to God, but he believed that he could not; that although the way of repentance was open to everyone else it was closed to him. He seemed to have this on very good authority, a voice coming from Heaven itself. But if we think about what Elisha ben Abuya heard, it did not tell him he was unable to repent, it told him not to repent. It told Elisha he should not try, but he misinterpreted that to mean that if he attempted to repent then he would be rejected. That was not what the voice said, because it is not true.

Elisha may have heard what he wanted to hear, but the truth is that if Elisha had decided to return to God sincerely and with contrition and resolution, God would have taken him back. The ultimate tragedy of Elisha ben Abuya is that he saw a closed door and thought it was locked. In fact, if he'd only pushed it a little, it would have opened up before him.

I am not sure God always wants us to knock at the door, but once we do knock, He has to open it for us. Sometimes that means we have to return to God in spite of God, but we can do it, and nothing can stop us. As Maimonides writes in his Laws of Repentance:

> A person may commit a great sin or many sins causing the judgement [to be that] his teshuvah will be held back.

Why does God hold back such a person's *teshuvah*, why does He get in the way of it taking place? Why does Maimonides not tell us that a wicked person's *teshuvah* is rejected? In fact, why does Maimonides tell us the exact opposite:

If a person performs repentance, then they achieve repentance and they have a place in the world to come.

The reason is that if a person, however distant, actually goes through the teshuvah process, it will be received and they will be forgiven and embraced. There are certainly very wicked people who never give a second thought to *teshuvah*, who never consider it, who regard it as laughable or absurd, or worst of all, unnecessary.

They might be the people that Maimonides is talking about. But anyone who entertains the notion, the possibility, of teshuvah has not lost the ability and will not lose the ability until the day of their death. If we make the decision at any point that we want to return we will be able to do so and God will take us back, and in Maimonides' words we will become *ahuv venechmad, karov veyadid:* beloved, dear, close and precious.

A Jew may choose to return to God or may choose not to, but we all have to know and deeply understand that we are able to. Even when the gates of Yom Kippur close the gates of God's love stay open.

There is a pair of bronze doors in Rome that stand at the entrance to the Pantheon. They were placed there by the Emperor Hadrian nineteen hundred years ago. They are four and half metres wide and seven and half metres high. They weigh eight and a half tonnes each, but they are so perfectly balanced they can be pushed open by a single person.

These High Holidays and this Yom Kippur let us not be intimidated by the great metal doors we see standing between us and our reconciliation with God. Let's walk up to those doors and push them open.

On Yom Kippur, What Does the Innocent Child Say?

Earl Schwartz

When, having eaten from the tree of knowledge, our eyes were opened, our gaze didn't first fall on our actions, but on what we now realised we are: "עירום/ערום." It was a deeply disconcerting sight, and we immediately attempted to cover it up. The word 'ערום,' which can be read as 'naked' or 'conniving,' first appears a few verses earlier, once in reference to human beings, and then again, to a snake.[1] The conventional rendering is that it is we humans who are naked, while the snake is calculating, but the text gives no indication that the term should be parsed this way, and when it is not, the cover-up is all the more revealing.

In his essay *What Is Man?* Martin Buber reflects on a "primal guilt" evoked by the call the furtive humans now hear: "Where are you?"[2] This first divine question, Buber concludes, echoes ever after in a second question heard "as soft and secret as though it came from myself: 'Where were you?' *That* is the cry of conscience."[3]

Our eyes opened, we cannot help but see that we are both vulnerable and crafty, but there is no moving on in the world that awaits us if that is all we see each time we open our eyes. And so, soon after, before being sent out of the Garden, God makes a gift for us: coverings. That our Creator would replace our futile fig leaves with pelt coats is perhaps the most poignant act of divine *chesed* in all of Tanakh. Prepared or not to answer that first question, God meets us where we are, with a parent's sheltering love for children leaving Eden.

Yom Kippur is rooted in the assumption that our own efforts alone cannot dispel the sense of guilt we bear as we move through the world, born not only of things we've done, but of who we come to know ourselves to be. We bear the responsibility for working to undo the consequences of our wrongful actions, but turning ourselves around/*teshuvah* is significantly different from receiving the gift of *kippurim*, which appears to be etymologically linked to 'cover.'[4] In Mishnah Tractate Yoma, focused on the latter, the word '*teshuvah*' is used for the first time in the 59th of 60 *mishnayot* in the tractate.

And so the description of Yom Kippur in early rabbinic sources as joyous. Not a special day for the ongoing work of righting through a relationship what we have done wrong in a relationship - every day is a day for reconciliation – but for *kippur*,[5] which alone can lead to the assurance that "*lif'nei* ה' *tit-haru*/ you will be made pure in God's presence."[6]

Not magic, but grace; not only forgiven in relationship, but miraculously *tahor* in fact. Through an honest accounting of who we are and the guilt we inevitably incur, our deeper, primal debts are covered. Like the coats we received leaving Eden, it is a gift, as is the note tucked in the pocket: "Now you can move on."

A covering, mended and refitted year by year; not for hiding, but for getting on with life.

The Abrahamic faiths, each in their own ways, have clung to this hope, but for Jews, the centre of gravity of Yom Kippur shifted in the wake of the destruction of the Temple. Kohein-mediated *kippur* focused on purging places and bodies of the shadow of death. On Yom Kippur this function was joined to moral renewal, and this theme now predominates. Sins once confessed over the desert-bound goat, are now evoked by a soft and secret "Where were you?" R. Elazar ben Azariah's counsel, appended to the close of Mishnah Yoma, that the purifying power of the day itself does not cover offences against a fellow human being unless the offender had first reached out to the offended and the breach healed, foreshadowed this transformation.

In these ways, Yom Kippur was rendered a counterpart to Rosh haShanah – Yom ha-Din/ Judgement Day – linked by ten days of *teshuvah.* But in the process, awareness of the remedial miracle has dimmed, while a primal awareness of our debt remains.

The innocence a court affirms on a yom din, but cannot definitively pronounce, is a muddled thing. In practice it goes no further than "not guilty." Yom Kippur isn't rooted in such a verdict. Sharing in the primal innocence that breaks the heart, the pureness nestled among the earliest of all memories, and relived in the innocence of the child whose eyes are not yet fully open to all that we are; a touch of the innocence of the unaware and unwary, that is the wondrous gift of Yom Kippur.

Tamah, ma hee omeret?

On Yom Kippur,
what does the innocent child say?
"Miracles happen."
כן יהי רצון

[1] The differing definitions and spellings may stem from two different roots, but given the oral basis of the narrative, the overlapping sound of the words is decisive. The assonance, along with the shared spelling in the first two instances, undoubtedly suggests a correlation.
[2] Genesis 3:9.
[3] M. Buber, *Between Man and Man* (Macmillan, 1965), 166.
[4] S. Brown, F. Driver, C. Briggs, *Hebrew and English Lexicon of the Old Testament* (Clarendon, 1975) 497.
[5] After noting that we are subject to judgement "every day, every hour, every moment," Louis Jacobs adds that setting aside a special day for repentance and communion with God provides for the power and inspiration that can come from finding oneself among many others who are similarly engaged. See L. Jacobs, *A Guide to Yom Kippur* (Jewish Chronicle Publications, 1957), 3-4.
[6] Lev. 16:30.

BIOGRAPHIES

Rachel Adelman is Associate Professor of Hebrew Bible at Boston's Hebrew College, where she also received ordination. She holds a Ph.D. in Hebrew Literature from the Hebrew University of Jerusalem, and is the author of *The Return of the Repressed: Pirqe de-Rabbi Eliezer and the Pseudepigrapha* (Brill 2009), based on her dissertation, and *The Female Ruse: Women's Deception and Divine Sanction in the Hebrew Bible* (Sheffield Phoenix, 2015), written under the auspices of the Women's Studies in Religion Program (WSRP) at Harvard.

Bradley Shavit Artson holds the Abner and Roslyn Goldstine Dean's Chair of the Ziegler School of Rabbinic Studies and is Vice President of American Jewish University. Rabbi Artson has long been a passionate advocate for social justice, human dignity, diversity and inclusion. He is also dean of the Zacharias Frankel College in Potsdam, Germany, ordaining Conservative rabbis for Europe. He is the author of 12 books and over 250 articles, most recently *Renewing the Process of Creation: A Jewish Integration of Science and Spirit.*

Harris Bor is a Research Fellow and Lecturer at the London School of Jewish Studies and a barrister specialising in international arbitration and commercial litigation. He holds a PhD in Theology from Cambridge University and received his rabbinic ordination from the Montefiore Endowment, London. His interests include intellectual history, Jewish philosophy and spirituality, and law and society. He is a Commissioner with the AI, Faith and Civil Society Commission, adviser to and board member of AI and Faith, and the author of *Staying Human, A Theology for the Age of Artificial Intelligence.*

Benjamin Elton has been Chief Minister of The Great Synagogue in Sydney, Australia since 2015. Born in Manchester, England, Rabbi Elton earned an MA in History at Queens' College, Cambridge and a PhD in Jewish History at Birkbeck, University of London. In addition to his 2014 book, Britain's Chief Rabbis and the Religious Character of Anglo-Jewry, 1880–1970, he has authored several articles on Anglo-Jewish and Australian Jewish religious history and is a Fellow of the Royal Historical Society of London.

Yaffa Epstein is the Senior Scholar and Educator in Residence at the Jewish Education Project. Formerly, she served as the Director of the Wexner Heritage Program at the Wexner Foundation, and the Director of Education, North America for the Pardes Institute of Jewish Studies. She has served on the faculties of Pardes, Yeshivat Maharat and the Drisha Institute. Rabba Epstein has taught in depth courses on Talmud, Rabbinic Literature, Jewish Pluralism, Jewish liturgy, Jewish leadership, and Women in Jewish Law. She received Orthodox Rabbinic Ordination from Yeshivat Maharat, earned an additional private Ordination from Rabbi Daniel Landes, holds a Law Degree from Bar-Ilan University, and studied at the Talmud Department at Hebrew University. She is the recipient of the prestigious Covenant Award which recognizes exceptional Jewish educators. Rabba Epstein has trained leaders, rabbis and educators from across the spectrum of Jewish denominations and is passionate about making Torah and Jewish learning accessible, exciting, and inclusive for all who wish to participate.

David Frankel is Associate Professor of Bible at the Schechter Institute of Jewish Studies. He has been on the faculty since 1992. He earned his PhD from the Hebrew University of Jerusalem under the direction of Prof. Moshe Weinfeld. His publications include *The Murmuring Stories of the Priestly School* and *The Land of Canaan and the Destiny of Israel.*

Jeremy Gordon is a rabbi at the New London Synagogue (Masorti) in London. He was ordained at JTS and is the author of *Spiritual Vagabondry*, co-author of *An Angel Called Truth and Other Tales* and authored the commentaries for the *Izzun Books Megilat Este*r, recently published by the very wonderful Izzun Books.

Steven Gotlib is Associate Rabbi at Mekor Habracha/ Center City Synagogue, having previously held a number of rabbinic positions in Ottawa, Toronto, and New York City. A graduate of Rutgers University, Rabbi Gotlib received ordination from the Rabbi Isaac Elchanan Theological Seminary at Yeshiva University (RIETS) as well as a Certificate in Mental Health Counseling from the Ferkauf School of Psychology in partnership with RIETS and a START Certificate in Spiritual Entrepreneurship from the Glean Network in partnership with Columbia Business School. He lives in Philadelphia with his wife and daughter.

Naomi Graetz taught English at Ben Gurion University of the Negev for 35 years. She is the author of *Unlocking the Garden: A Feminist Jewish Look at the Bible, Midrash and God; The Rabbi's Wife Plays at Murder; S/He Created Them: Feminist Retellings of Biblical Stories; Forty Years of Being a Feminist Jew.* She teaches regular classes about Bible and Modern Midrash from a feminist perspective on Zoom. She writes a weekly blog at the Times of Israel. Her book

Silence is Deadly: Judaism Confronts Wifebeating has been translated into Hebrew and is forthcoming with Carmel Press at the end of 2024.

Chaim (Harvey) J. Hames is a professor of history at Ben-Gurion University of the Negev (BGU), in Beer-Sheva, Israel and the incumbent of the David Berg and Family Chair in European History. He has been Rector of BGU since 2018. Hames' research focuses on mediaeval history, with a particular interest in inter-religious encounters, particularly between Christianity, Judaism, and Islam. He also works on religious conversion, inter-religious polemics, mysticism, philosophy, apocalypticism, and magic.

Tova Hartman is the founding Dean of Humanities and Social Sciences at Ono Academic College in Israel. She is the author of several books including *Men With Broken Hearts* (Kinneret Zmora-Bitan Dvir, 2022; Hebrew), *Are You Not a Man of God? Devotion, Betrayal, and Social Criticism in Jewish Tradition* (Oxford, 2014), and *Feminism Encounters Traditional Judaism: Resistance and Accommodation* (Brandeis, 2007), which won the National Jewish Book Award. Her first book, *Appropriately Subversive: Modern Mothers in Traditional Religions* (Harvard, 2002), brought her into the world of interfaith research and communal action, where she maintains a vital presence as a lecturer and participant at conferences relating to gender, religion, and social change. She is completing a new book, *Loss, Resentment, Revenge, and Repair,* set for release in Hebrew this year. Tova is one of the founders of Kehillat Shira Hadasha, the first partnership synagogue in Jerusalem. She has a doctorate in human development and psychology from Harvard University.

Herzl Hefter is the founder at Rosh Beit Midrash Har'el in memory of Belda Kaufman Lindenbaum, in Jerusalem. He is a graduate of Yeshiva University where he learned under the tutelage of Rabbi Yosef Dov Soloveichik, and received smicha from Rabbi Aharon Lichtenstein at Yeshivat Har Etzion where he studied for ten years. He has written numerous articles related to modernity and Hasidic thought. His Torah essays and online *shiurim* can be accessed at *www.har-el.org.*

Shai Held is a philosopher, theologian, and Bible scholar. He is President and Dean at the Hadar Institute. He received the prestigious Covenant Award for Excellence in Jewish Education, and has been named multiple times by Newsweek as one of the fifty most influential rabbis in America and by the Jewish Daily Forward as one of the fifty most prominent Jews in the world. Rabbi Held is the author of *Abraham Joshua Heschel: The Call of Transcendence* (2013), *The Heart of Torah* (2017), and *Judaism is About Love* (2024) and he is the host of Hadar's newest podcast, Answers WithHeld.

Deborah Kahn-Harris is the Principal of Leo Baeck College in London, where she also teaches Hebrew Bible. She holds a PhD in Bible from the University of Sheffield. She previously served as the Teaching Fellow in Judaism at the School for Oriental and African Studies, University of London. Her most recent book is *Polyamory and Reading the Book of Ruth.*

Samuel Klein is Director of Jewish Engagement for the Jewish Federation of Greater Seattle. Previously he has been Chief Jewish Life Officer at the JCC of San Francisco, Director of Re-Imagining Jewish Education Through Art at Yeshiva University Museum, New York, Executive Director of the Bronfman Jewish Education

Centre in Montreal, and led the Coexistence Trust, a think-tank and NGO providing consultation and training in the areas of campus leadership and inter-communal dialogue. A lecturer and writer on religion and the visual arts, Rabbi Klein holds Masters degrees in Theology from Cambridge University and History of Art from University College London and trained as a teaching artist at Lincoln Center for the Performing Arts.

Joel Levy became the rabbi of Kol Nefesh Masorti in London in September 2001. He is Director of the Conservative Yeshiva, Jerusalem, where he is also active in inter-denominational and inter-faith work.

Natasha Mann is a rabbi at the New London Synagogue in London. She was ordained at the Ziegler School of Rabbinic Studies in 2019 and prior to that, achieved a first class honours degree in Theology from Heythrop College, University of London.

Francis Nataf is a Jerusalem-based thinker, writer, educator, and translator. He has held senior educational positions in many different contexts in Israel and the United States, including as Educational Director at the David Cardozo Academy, but has more recently focused on teaching and writing. He has written a highly acclaimed five-volume modern Torah commentary, published countless articles, and serves as Associate Editor for the *Jewish Bible Quarterly*. He teaches Tanakh at Midreshet Rachel v'Chaya and is the Translation and Research Specialist at Sefaria, for whom he has written many new original translations, including of such classics as *Sefer HaChinukh, Sha'arei Teshuva, Derekh Hashem,* and *Chovat HaTalmidim.*

Daniel Nevins is Head of School at Golda Och Academy in West Orange, New Jersey. He previously served as Pearl Resnick Dean of the JTS Rabbinical School, and as Senior Rabbi of Adat Shalom Synagogue in Farmington Hills, MI. A graduate of Harvard College and JTS, he has been a member of the Rabbinical Assembly's Committee on Jewish Law and Standards since 1999. Rabbi Nevins's volume of responsa, *Torah and Technology: Circuits, Cells, and the Sacred Path*, was published by Izzun Books in 2024.

Jeremy Rosen was educated at Cambridge University in England and Mir Yeshiva in Jerusalem. He has practiced as an orthodox rabbi, as principal of Carmel College in the UK, and as professor at the Faculty for Comparative Religion in Antwerp, Belgium. He has written and lectured extensively in the UK and the US, where he now resides.

Earl Schwartz is retired from the Hamline University (St. Paul, Minnesota) religion faculty, where he was also director of Hamline's Social Justice Studies program. He is the author of *Moral Development: A Practical Guide for Jewish Teachers*, and co-author with Rabbi Barry Cytron of *When Life Is In the Balance: Life and Death Decisions in Light of the Jewish Tradition.* His most recent book is *Arc of the Covenant: Jewish Educational Success on the Upper Mississippi.*

Yiscah Smith is a thought leader and spiritual activist who teaches Jewish spiritual texts and contemplative practice at the Pardes Institute of Jewish Studies and at Applied Jewish Spirituality. She has also founded and directs Conscious Community Nachlaot, an organization in Jerusalem that hosts Shabbat in-person spiritual gatherings, virtual guided meditation sits and spiritual text classes. Her forthcoming book, *Planting Seeds of* *the Divine: Torah Commentaries to Cultivate Your Spiritual Practice*, published jointly by the University of Nebraska Press and the Jewish Publication Society, will be released in 2025.

Jeremy Tabick is the Content Manager and faculty at Hadar, where he teaches, curates, and edits Hadar's content—both online and in print—and Project Zug courses. Jeremy received his PhD in Talmud at JTS. He graduated from the University of Manchester with a Masters in Physics, and is an alumnus of Yeshivat Hadar and the Conservative Yeshiva in Jerusalem.

Tzemah Yoreh is one of the intellectual leaders of Jewish humanism and the head of the City Congregation in New York city. He attended the Hebrew University of Jerusalem, where he obtained his Ph.D. in biblical criticism in 2004. He earned a second Ph.D. in Ancient Wisdom Literature from the University of Toronto for the joy of studying ancient text.

Jonathan Wittenberg is Senior Rabbi of Masorti Judaism and Rabbi of the New North London Synagogue. He is a leading writer and thinker on Judaism. He is a co-founder of Eco-Synagogue and deeply engaged in environmental issues. He teaches and speaks widely, including on Radio 4's Thought for the Day. He was appointed OBE in the 2024 New Year Honours for services to the Jewish community and interfaith relations. His most recent book is *Listening for God in Torah and Creation: A Weekly Encounter with Conscience and Soul.*

EDITORS

Adam Zagoria-Moffet is the rabbi of St. Albans Masorti Synagogue in Hertfordshire, the Director of the Louis Jacobs Foundation, and the Editor-in-Chief of Izzun Books. He received ordination from the Jewish Theological Seminary of America, where he also completed a Masters in Jewish Thought.

Simon Eder is Education Director of the Louis Jacobs Foundation. He hosts the podcast *Jewish Quest* in which he interviews leading scholars on the weekly Torah portion, drawing audiences from around the world. His book, *Jewish Angle of the Week,* was a compilation of his blog posts during Covid lockdown. He is one of the founders of the Jewish community in Dubai. He graduated from the University of Cambridge with a degree in Theology and Religious Studies.

Louis Jacobs Foundation

louisjacobs.org | jewishquest.org | booksof.louisjacobs.org

IZZUN BOOKS

VISIT US AT IZZUNBOOKS.COM

Printed in Great Britain
by Amazon

47635597R00096